Dylan Thomas was born in Swansea on 27 October 1914. After leaving school he worked briefly on the *South Wales Evening Post* before embarking on his literary career in London. Not only a poet, he wrote short stories, film scripts, features and radio plays, the most famous being *Under Milk Wood*. On 9 November 1953, shortly after his 39th birthday, he collapsed and died in New York City. In 1982 a memorial stone to commemorate him was unveiled in Poets' Corner in Westminster Abbey.

Also available from W&N

A Dylan Thomas Treasury
The Best of Dylan Thomas
The Loud Hill of Wales
Portrait of the Artist as a Young Dog
Under Milk Wood
Selected Poems
Collected Letters
Collected Poems
Collected Stories

I THINK OF YOU ALWAYS ALL THE TIME

Love Letters

DYLAN THOMAS

Previously published as
The Love Letters of Dylan Thomas

W&N
WEIDENFELD & NICOLSON

First published as *The Love Letters of Dylan Thomas*
in Great Britain in 2001 by J. M. Dent
This paperback edition published in 2026 by Weidenfeld & Nicolson,
an imprint of The Orion Publishing Group Ltd
Carmelite House, 50 Victoria Embankment
London EC4Y 0DZ

An Hachette UK Company

The authorised representative in the EEA is Hachette Ireland,
8 Castlecourt Centre, Dublin 15, D15 XTP3, Ireland
(email: info@hbgi.ie)

1 3 5 7 9 10 8 6 4 2

A CIP catalogue record for this book is
available from the British Library.

ISBN (Mass Market Paperback) 978 1 3996 3787 9
ISBN (Ebook) 978 1 7802 2894 5

Printed in Great Britain by Clays Ltd, Elcograf, S.p.A.

FSC www.fsc.org MIX Paper | Supporting responsible forestry FSC® C104740

www.weidenfeldandnicolson.co.uk
www.orionbooks.co.uk

Introduction

'The idea of myself, sitting in the open window, in my shirt, and imagining myself as some Jehovah of the West, is really odd. If I were some Apollo, it would be different. As a matter of fact, I am a little person with much untidy hair.'

This collection is just a short selection from the letters of the poet Dylan Thomas. In his short life, Dylan Thomas wrote many letters. Whether he was writing from his home in Wales as a young man, to friends in the wilder world, or writing home from abroad as a famous poet, his letters chart the course of his life in a way that is almost incomprehensible to the lost email generation. In almost all his letters, there is art: pleading, cajoling, amusing, charming. And poetry. But the most beautiful of his letters are the ones he wrote to the women in his life, to his wife Caitlin and other lovers. He used his letters, as his poetry, to convey an immediate and emotional effect, binding the reader by the spell of his words rather than coolly delivering his message – although the message is often clear.

Dylan Thomas was born in Swansea in 1914. His first published collection was *Eighteen Poems* which appeared at the end of 1934 when he was only 20. He married Caitlin Macnamara in 1936, the same year that his second volume, *Twenty-Five Poems* appeared. He died, almost certainly of alcohol abuse, in New York in 1953. He was not yet forty. The following year, *Under Milk Wood*, a radio script about a Welsh seaside village upon which he had been working off and on for ten years, was published.

The Collected Letters of Dylan Thomas, in a revised edition edited by Paul Ferris, is again available from J. M. Dent.

'Now the threads of halfremembered ideas, the fragments of halfremembered facts blow about in my head. I can write today – only awkwardly & uneasily, nib akimbo. And I want to write so differently: in flowing, unaffected prose: with all the heat of my heart, or, if that is cold, with all the clear intellectual heat of the head.'

PAMELA HANSFORD JOHNSON

Pamela Hansford Johnson wrote an admiring letter to Dylan Thomas after seeing a poem of his in a small magazine. She was his first real girlfriend, although he sometimes boasted of earlier encounters, including one in the back of a van when he was fifteen. Pamela lived with her mother in South London and worked in a bank. She was also an aspiring writer. Dylan at the time, just eighteen when they began to write to each other, was living with his parents in Swansea. They didn't get to meet until the spring of the following year. Their letters were full of poetry, of their future life together, of Dylan's health (he fancied himself consumptive and certainly smoked and drank a great deal, even then). The end of the affair when it came was precipitated by Dylan's avowed infidelity with an unnamed woman in Wales. Pamela forgave him but the romance was over. She went on to become a novelist and married a novelist, Lord (C. P.) Snow.

September, 1933 Blaen-Cwm Llangain near Carmarthen

Beginning this letter in the way I do, removes the necessity of using the formal, 'madam', the stiff, 'Miss Johnson', (rather ambiguous but entirely unmeant), and the impudent, 'Pamela', (also ambiguous, also unmeant). It removes a similar obstacle in your case.

If it is 'gruesome' to reply to letters, then I am as much

of a ghoul as you are. I return frequently, in the characterless scrawl God and a demure education gave me.

Incidentally, when you reply to this – and let it be long and soon – don't write to the above address. It is merely a highly poetical cottage where I sometimes spend week-ends. Reply to my nasty, provincial address.

Thank you for the poems. Mr Neuburg has paid you a large and almost merited compliment. 'One of the few exquisite word-artists of our day', needs little praise or abuse from me. But, still, I must compliment you upon 'The Nightingale', by far the best of the three poems. Comparing that with the 'Sea Poem for G', one of the most perfect examples of bloody verse I have ever seen, and with other Referee poems, is like comparing Milton with Stilton. I like the other two poems you sent me, but not as much, and the first stanza of 'Prothalamium', I don't like at all. Too many adjectives, too much sugar. And the fifth and sixth lines are pure cliché. 'I write from the heart', said a character in some novel I've forgotten. 'You write', was the reply, 'from the bowels as after a strong emetic.' Not that I apply that rude remark to 'Prothalamium'; I'm quoting not because of it but for the sake of it.

Of course you are not an agèd virgin. But many of the contributors to the Poet's Corner are, and woo the moon for want of a better bedfellow. I can't agree with you that the majority of the Referee poems are good. With a few exceptions they are nauseatingly bad. Yours are among the exceptions, of course. Do you remember a poem called '1914' printed a couple of weeks ago? Do you remember the 'Sea Poem'? Do you remember those few diabetic lines about an Abyssinian cat? What did you think of last week's 'Blue Gum Tree'? That is a real test of taste. Like that, you like anything. It would be hard to realise the number of people bluffed into believing 'Blue Gum Tree' to be a good poem. Its sprawling formlessness they would call, 'modern', its diction, 'harsh but effective', and some of its single lines, such as, 'The cloth of silver over a white balustrade', would send them into some sort of colourful rapture. In reality, the formlessness is the outcome of entire prosodical incompetence, the diction is not even tailor-made but ready-to-wear, and the 'colourful' lines are like cheap, vermilion splotches on a tenthrate music-hall backcloth.

In the very interesting copy you sent me of the first Poet's Corner, it is explained that when, during any week, no poetry is received, the best *verse* would be printed. That would be perfectly all right if it did happen. But the pretentious palming off of *doggerel* (not even verse) as 'arty' poetry is too much.

It was on the same grounds that I objected to 'Poet's Corner' as a title. There was a time when only poets were called poets. Now anyone with an insufficient knowledge of the English language, a Marie Corelli sentiment, and a couple of 'bright' images to sprinkle over the lines, is called a poet. He can't even leave his excretion in a private spot. They give him a public 'Corner' to leave it in. (A vulgar metaphor! I hope you don't object.)

This is in no way a biased or personal attack. It's the general principles of the thing I like to use as Aunt Sallies. Pray God I, too, am not 'arty'. A physical pacifist and a mental militarist, I can't resist having a knock – or even a blow at a dead horse – when all I put my faith in is utterly contradicted. I put my faith in poetry, and too many poets deny it.

To return to *your* poetry, (you must excuse my slight soap-box attitude): It shows a tremendous passion for words, and a real knowledge of them. Your grasp of form and your handling of metre is among the best I know today. And – the main thing – your thoughts are worth expressing. Have you written a great deal? When do you write? I'm interested to know all sorts of things like that, and to see some more.

What I like about your poems is that they *state*, not contradict, that *they create* not destroy. Poem after poem, recording, in sickening detail, the wrinkles on the author's navel, fill the contemporary journals, poem after poem recording, none too clearly, the chaos of to-day. Out of chaos they make nothing, but, themselves part of the post-war carnage, fade away like dead soldiers. So much new verse (do you know 'New Verse'?) can be summarised into, 'Well, there's been a hell of a war; it's left us in a mess; what the hell are we going to do about it?' The answer is fairly obvious. But is it worth writing about? No, you answer in a loud voice, or at least I hope you do. You are not like that, and your 'not-ness' alone is worth all the superlatives at my command.

So you are the same age as myself. You say one has enough time, when one is 21, to be modest. One has enough time ahead, too, to regret one's immodesty. The more I think of my Referee poem the less I like it. The idea of myself, sitting in the open window, in my shirt, and imagining myself as some Jehovah of the West, is really odd. If I were some Apollo, it would be different. As a matter of fact, I am a little person with much untidy hair.

With this letter you will find two poems of mine. I am sending them to show you, or to hope to show you, that I can do much better than you think from what you have seen of mine. Incidentally, I'd better mention that the poem starting, 'No food suffices', is, though complete in itself, the woman's lament from an unfortunately unfinished play. I think this needs mention; references in the poem would otherwise cast aspersions on the nature of my sex. The second poem you may not like at all; it is distinctly unfashionable.

After my violent outburst against the Referee poets, you'll probably read *my* two poems with a stern & prejudiced eye. I hope you don't, and I hope you like them. Whether you do or not, tell me.

Can I keep your poems for a little longer?

Dylan Thomas

P.S. The Woman poem is to be printed in the Adelphi. I can't resist adding that, because I like the magazine so much. The Jesus poem is probably to be printed in T. S. Eliot's Criterion, though, as a rule, the Criterion doesn't print any metaphysic verse at all. I mention the 'C' for the same reason that I mention the 'A'.
P.P.S. I am staying, as you see, in Carmarthenshire & have forgotten to bring your address with me. I am trusting to luck that 13 is the right number. If it is, you will read this explanation. If it isn't, you won't. So there was no point at all in writing it. *D.T.*

March, 1934

My dear Pamela (I may call you that, mayn't I?)

So glad to have your letter. What a nice hand you have. You must write to me again some time. I do *so* love receiving *intellectual* letters, don't you? It gives you a sort of – how shall I put it – a sort of stimulus, don't you find? And when one is plucking one's own little flowers from the Garden of Poesy (such a lovely phrase, don't you think. It was told to me by a Mr Wheeble), it helps, nay invigorates one to fresh horticultural efforts, to know that far away from one is yet another soul searching for Beauty ('Truth is Beauty', you know, as Keats so aptly put it) in those Evergreen Haunts.

And my dear, how can I tell you in words – words! ah, frail words! such gossamer cups they be! – the emotions your prosepoems inspired in my bosom. (I have often thought, haven't you, that whereas the Upper Classes have bosoms the Working Classes almost invariably have breasts.) Those dainty pieces smacked – ah, false pen! See how you play your gay little tricks with me! – of a loveliness which even I, humble in my devotion to the Great God

Pan (Elizabeth Browning, you remember) have sought after through many sunny hours. So sweetly indeed did they fall upon my ears (Shakespeare, I think, but if Sir Walter Scott I stand corrected) that I have arranged with Mrs Grimmfluf that you address our next weekly meeting of the Ladies Culture Guild on 'Inspirations I Have Received'. Is this too personal a title? Perhaps I could arrange for you to speak on 'The Sexual Habits of Moths'. Our Guild is *so* entranced with Natural History. *Do* write to me again. Who knows, maybe I shall let you see my little volume of verse. I call it, 'Thru' Hull with the Muses'.

Yours,
Sinfonietta Bradshaw (Miss)

Kind Lady,

Hearin yew ar a poitess and travel on the tramz I hav beene wonderin if you would care to spare me a 2/6. I have a mutual perculeirity with yew, kind lady; I, too, travel on the tramz, though, being a bachelor of sum 57 years I am no poitess. By perfession I am a Female Impersonator, and I were silk nex to my skin.

Thankin yew for the 2/6, I hope,

I am,
Lesley Pough

Dear Sir,

We are sorry but we must return your poem. You are, we assume, under a misapprehension. Our offices are the offices of the London Mercury-Manufacturers Association, & not of the Mercury Periodical edited, we believe, by Sir John Sitwell.

Yours Faithfully,
Rod, Pole, & Perch Ltd

Dear Madam,

Will you do us the honour of accepting this small Rhyming Dictionary, a tribute of our sincerest admiration. (Move up the car, please!)

From,

The L.C.C. Tramway Workers Union

Thank God, now I can get a word in. You'll be interested to know that the B.B.C. have banned my poetry. After my poem in the Listener ('Light Breaks Where No Sun Shines') the editor received a host of letters, all complaining of the disgusting obscenity in two of the verses. One of the bits they made a fuss about was:

'Nor fenced, nor staked, the *gushers* of the sky
Spout to the *rod* divining in a smile
The *oil* of tears.'

The little smut-hounds thought I was writing a copulatory anthem. In reality, of course, it was a metaphysical image of rain & grief. I shall never darken Sir John Reith's doors again, for all my denials of obscenity were disregarded. Jesus, what are we up against, Pam?

The poem you didn't like, along with 'When the galactic sea was sucked', & a new poem which I'm sending you, is to be printed in the April New Verse. That particular poem isn't as bad as you think. There is no reason at all why I should not write of gunmen, cinemas & pylons if what I have to say necessitates it. Those words & images were essential. Just as some have a complex in regard to lambs & will never mention them even though lambs are necessary for their thought, you, my Christina, refuse to look a pylon in the face. I wasn't conceding anything. I wanted gunmen, and, shatter my hams (your oath, but such a wonderful one that you mustn't be allowed to have it all for yourself) I bloody well had them. Ha!

I'll be up as early as possible on Saturday, but don't hold anything up (I don't mean hold up a flag or an old man's adenoids in a bottle: you know what I mean), because I mayn't be able to leave Swansea until Friday night. More than probably I shall, of course, but I'm telling you this in case . . . It's no good me saying I'm looking forward to seeing you again. You know how much I am.

What are we going to do? Smile darkly over the fire?

I want to see Congreve's 'Love for Love' at Sadler's Wells, if it's still on. Will you come? Or is there something else you'd prefer to see. There's the 'Country Wife'; that should bring out your best bawdy laugh. Find out if 'Juno & the Paycock' is still running. It isn't in the West End, I know, but it may be in some obscure theatre.

What a chatty little letter this. Nothing but facts. It must be – it is – the effect of this pedantic day. The sky looks like the graph of a heavenly calculation.

No, I haven't been doing anything I shouldn't. I have smoked only two cigarettes since I last saw you. You can't – yes, you can – realise how terrible it has been to give them up. I've chain-smoked for nearly five years; which must have done me a lot of good. I am allowed a pipe – mild tobacco, not too much. That keeps me alive, though I hate it like hell. I take walks in the morning and pretend there's a sun in these disappointed skies. I even go without a coat (sometimes) in this cold weather, & tread be-jumpered over the sheepy fields.

I've told you, I think, about the coughing sheep that plague my life. In front of my nice little villa is a field where bankrupt farmers pasture their animals before the time of the slaughter house. It's hard to believe how many of those doomed creatures are consumptive. Good old meat-eaters. In a week that particularly diseased sheep that keeps me awake half the night with its centenarian coughs will be done to death, cut up in various saleable lengths, and hung on hooks in butchers' windows. Some sweet little child will develop a sore throat one of these days, or suddenly his lung will break up like a plate (not a Bell plate). So much for the carnivorous. One day I shall undoubtedly turn into a potato. You won't like me then. And, on that day of Transformation, I certainly shan't like you, salt rasher of bacon!

I like to be tidy-minded, but I so rarely am. Now the threads of halfremembered ideas, the fragments of half-remembered facts, blow about in my head. I can write today only awkwardly & uneasily, nib akimbo. And I want to write so differently: in glowing, unaffected prose: with all the heat of my heart, or, if that is cold, with all the clear intellectual heat of the head.

There were no shear-marks visible in my last letter for the reason that I had cut out nothing. I never shall in my letters, though the uncut material may, when I think back on it, hurt me very much. And how horribly easy it is to be hurt. I am being hurt all day, & hurt by the tiniest & most subtle things. So on goes the everyday armour, and the self, even the wounded self, is hidden from so many. If I pull down the metals, don't shoot, dear. Not even with a smile or a pleasant smile or a rehearsed smile. (Like a speech from a Russian drama. Look, little Ivanivitch, there are bodies in the Volga. One is your little aunt Pamela. Go give her a snow-cold kiss. No, O little wretch, that is a dead postman. That is your auntie, the one with the poem in her teeth.)

What a biased child! 'Dolphined' is *your* word. Nothing shall take it away from you. All my words are your words (cue). The only reason I never finished the poem in which *your* word originally appeared was because I failed utterly to make it good enough. You are with me when I write (cue).

And now I shall rise from the lovely fire, jam my hat hard & painfully on my head, & go out into the grey day. I am strong, strong as a circus horse. I am going to walk, alone and stern, over the miles of grey hills at the top of this my hill. I shall call at a public house & drink beer with Welshspeaking labourers. Then I shall walk back over the hills again, alone & stern, covering up a *devastating* melancholy & a tugging, tugging weakness with a look of fierce & even Outpost-of-the-Empire determination & a seven-league stride. Strength! (And I'm damned if I want to go out at all. I want to play discords on the piano, write silly letters or sillier verses, sit down under the piano & cry Jesus to the mice.)

If *I* had money I would go round the world, looking for somewhere where the sun was always shining, beautiful & near to the sea. And there I should build me a house as splendid as Keawe's, so that people should call it the house of light. All day there should be music, and olive-skinned virgins, bearing wine in lotus-coloured bowls, should wait on my littlest want. Women with the voices of harps should read to me all day long. And one day, leaping up from my scented couch, I should cry, 'For Christ's sake give me a tram'.

May 9, 1934

Yesterday I received from Southampton a small, round tin of Tooth Powder, enclosed, in an explanatory note, at the request of a Mrs Johnson of Battersea Rise. 'Eucryl destroys germs in every part of the mouth.' Was that the intention of your mother's much-to-be-thanked request? Or perhaps you sent it after my ringworm poem, in order that I may clean my mouth out with great thoroughness? Give my love to your mother, and thank her for the Powder. Whether it will destroy the germs or not, I cannot possibly say. I hope not. I admire germs. And, if I remember, I shall bring a few more than usually bawdy paragraphs into this letter to satisfy their lecherous itches.

And, while I remember, too, let me raise one nasty growl

about your unparalleled bitchiness in pinching my letter to the Neuburg. I wrote a stony, non-committal letter to him, received your pathetic appeal, and immediately tore the old effusion up and posted off a charming, Micawberish affair. And don't you go about jeering at my Old School Tie. I hate Old School Ties. I haven't got one. I shall now attempt to light a Russian cigarette in a most rakish manner, and look all sexy at the mantelpiece. But it doesn't work. I am fated to be British under my Russian exterior. But don't always point at my Tie. Just pretend it isn't there. Anyway, it was a sweet letter, and, if nothing else, I meant what I said about Pamela Johnson, though if I had had any idea that she would see the letter, I would have introduced a long and dirty paragraph all about her nasty little moist-nosed muse.

Again I am unwell. Melodramatic introduction, reminiscent of some wheezy Shylock, to a page of remorse and self pity. But no, it shall not be. Even more melodramatic. Sir Jasper Murgatroyd enters through the trapdoor with a snarl, and immediately opens his waistcoat and distributes, from his navel, Empire Marketing Board pamphlets on 'The Caul of the Colonies'. To put it plainly – it is an intellectual impossibility to put anything plainly – I feel about as much use [*words deleted*] (a sudden puritanism makes me delete this. Very indecent). (I am trying very hard to deny the Tooth Powder, and to devote all my bawdy and soul to the composition of Old Tin Kettle innuendoes. But it fails. This May morning is un-naturally church. The birds sing the Ave Maria. My germs tell me that Ave Maria sounds like a sexual disease. I whisper 'Poonah' to them, and display an invisible gout. They vanish.) But I am ill, ill as hell. I have had a headache for a fortnight, and haven't slept for longer than that. I've lost all hope of ever going to sleep again. I lie in the dark and think. I think of God and Death and Triangles. I think of you a lot. But neither You nor the Triangles can make me sleep. I've drugged myself up to the eyelids. I have a little box of tablets with an instruction on the cover not to take, on any account, more than three. I take nine, and still I remain awake. I have tried everything. I have tried getting drunk. I have tried keeping sober. I have counted sheep and bathchairs. I have read till I can't see any more. I have tried completely under the bedclothes & on top of the bedclothes, right way up, wrong way up, with pyjamas, without pyjamas. A good idea, of course, is to gas yourself just a *little* bit. But I can't think how that's going to be done.

No more. Darling, send me to sleep. No more. Perpetually pathetic, these daft little notes of mine can serve no purpose but to show you, again and again, how much I need you.

And no Mediterranean for me. I'd love the sun, and I'd love the places the sun would take me to. But it's all useless, for, when I came back, I'd be just where I was before I went away – a little less pale perhaps, but as green as ever as to what I must do in this dull, grey country, & how one little colour must be made out of you and me. The chromosomes, the colour bodies that build towards the cells of these walking bodies, have a god in them that doesn't care a damn for the howls of our brains. He's a wise, organic god, moving in a seasonable cycle in the flesh, always setting and putting right what our howls at the astrologer's stars and the destiny of the sun leads us on to. If we listen to him, we're O.K. And he tells me, 'Don't you go away now. You stick to your unamiable writings and your never-to-be-popular morbidities. You stick as near as you can to what you love.' So no trampsteamer up a blue sea for me. Give me Pamela & a Chatterton attic. Enough for the likes of me, and too much, too, for God knows why she loves this idiot writing & writing, precious as a herring, on this Old School paper.

It must be this ecclesiastical morning that drives me into such stagey melancholia. And so, by cunningly sitting in a room looking over the east of Swansea chimney pots, I avoid the sun and all the priestcraft of May. I sit and devour the brick walls with my eyes, hoping to draw out a little of the masons' opium that, hot from their foul pipes, cemented these breeding huts together. But the room is stuffy, filled with the tobacco smoke it shouldn't be filled with & my naughty thoughts that leap, like Tom Warner's, from clinical observatories in Vienna to syphilitic cabarets in Buenos Aires, from Builth Wells to Chimborazo, from the altitudes of poetical ideals to the rhyming of 'catalepsy' and 'autopsy'.

I shall have nothing to send you. The old fertile days are gone, and now a poem is the hardest and most thankless act of creation. I have written a poem since my last letter, but it is so entirely obscure that I dare not let it out even unto the eyes of such a kind and commiserating world as yours. I am getting more obscure day by day. It gives me now a *physical* pain to write poetry. I feel all my muscles contract as I try to drag out, from the whirlpooling words around my everlasting ideas of the importance of death on the living, some connected words that will explain how the starry system of the dead is seen, ordered as in the grave's sky, along the orbit of a foot or a flower. But when the words do come, I pick them so thoroughly of their *live* associations that only the *death* in the words remains. And I could scream, with real, physical pain, when a line of mine is seen naked on paper & seen to be as meaningless as a Sanskrit limerick. I shall never be understood. I think I shall send no more poetry away, but write stories alone. All day yesterday I was working, as hard as a navvy, on six lines of a poem. I finished them, but had, in the labour of them, picked and cleaned them so much that nothing but their barbaric sounds remained. Or if I did write a line, 'My dead upon the orbit of a rose', I saw that 'dead' did not mean 'dead', 'orbit' not 'orbit' & 'rose' most certainly not 'rose'. Even 'upon' was a syllable too many, lengthened for the inhibited reason of rhythm. My lines, *all* my lines, are of the tenth intensity. They are not the words that express what I want to express; they are the only words I can find that come near to expressing a half. And that's no good. I'm a freak user of words, not a poet. That's really the truth. No self-pity there. A freak *user* of words, not a poet. That's terribly true.

> 'I'll not be a fool like the nightingale
> Who sits up till midnight without any ale,
> Making a noise with his nose,'

is a quotation I write down for no reason at all. Neither do I feel it to be correct. For I'll be a fool like the hyena, sitting up till dawn without any pleasure, making a noise with his guts.

This is out of mood with the day. I should be writing some sunny paragraphs, imagining in the words for you a green and blue expanse of Welsh country where the cattle, in accordance with all conventions, 'low', where the lambs 'frisk', and the glassy streams 'babble' or 'tumble' according to the rhyme. I'll walk this afternoon, and, perhaps, in the late night, when I write to you again, the nearsummer loveliness will have gone into me so deeply that all the clowning and the pretentious stomachraking of the last two pages will be nothing but an echo that refuses to 'ring' in your ears or an odour that refuses to 'waft' to your nose.

But, before I go out, very lonely and quite twice as pale & haggard as usual – I hardly weigh anything at all, eight stone or under now –, into my Gower bays, there are several matter of fact things in your last letter which I want to answer.

Now Orage, though a very pleasant and very sincere man, is known to be almost entirely lacking in taste. He runs the literary sections of the New English Weekly by a system of filing. He has in his office literally hundreds of poems and short sketches and stories. Most of them are bad, but that doesn't matter. It's quantity with him, not quality, that counts. And week by week one or two of those stories and poems are taken down from their dusty shelves and printed. You just wait your turn, and then in you go. So there's really very little satisfaction in having anything printed in Orage's paper. He doesn't pay *at all*, and the standard he sets is so low that it's hardly flattering to be accepted by him. He goes in for mediocrity. 'Headline', whatever its faults – and I begin to suspect that its main faults, at the moment, maybe my fault – is not mediocre, and not original enough – in subject, at least, – to startle him into an acceptance. I've no idea where you can plant 'Headline'. Its matter, I should imagine, would be too ordinary for 'New Stories', which deals with rather out-of-the-way affairs. 'The London Mercury' might like 'A Man Had A Monkey', though I believe they keep you waiting rather a long time before they reply. The 'Everyman' prints stories. So does 'John O'London'; but, for the last, the more conventional the better. I'll have a look at some more of the magazines littered about the house. I can't remember the name of the story, but the one about the watch, the little girl, and the nasty old gentleman, is more of a *commercial* effort than any I can think of of yours. And, though you'll probably squeal to heaven at the suggestion, you might do worse than send it to a paper such as 'Nash's'. There are scores of papers like that, above the standard of the 'Strand' & 'Pearsons', that *might* stretch their standards of taste sufficiently to allow admittance to your cheery little story. And have you sent any poems to J. C. Squire? And have you sent to Harriet Monroe? And what about a mild (very mild) poem to Frank Kendon, of John O'London's. He printed a terribly weak, watery little thing of mine – I've never shown it to you – last week (Saturday May 5). These do seem dreadfully lowbrow suggestions. But they're not derogatory. Far from it. But you've struck such a curious *medium* in your poetry lately that publication becomes very difficult; there are so few medium papers left. By that I don't mean 'middlebrow' or anything like that. But you've brought 'conventional' poetry, descendent from Tennyson & the middle Victorians, to a point of near-perfection, and any modern, even any *alive* influence, is absent. So that editors of most periodicals are rather troubled at your poetry, for most of the editors (&, unfortunately, the editresses) look at the influences first and the individuality afterwards. If a poem, in the John Donne descendency, is fairly good, they print it; if very good, in the Tennyson descendency, they refuse to. What they never realise – they cannot, of course, being, principally, caterers for the fashionable taste of the moment, and a taste which has spat Tennyson out & sucked up the good & the bad of John Donne in large mouthfuls – is that the convention, the heredity, of the poem doesn't matter a farthing. It's the individuality of the poet, an individuality that owes nothing to the Jacobeans or the Victorians, that really matters. If you, still (& inevitably) retaining the old Johnson individuality, were to tack on to your poems the conscious influence of Donne, Tourneur, Traherne or Manley Hopkins, you'd get published all over the place & be the moment's wow in every public salon. But you're not going to do that, because you realise that it's worthless, & that what Jack Common (entirely ignorant of everything outside intellectual socialism) refused for the Adelphi is far more valuable than most of the Donne-fathered babies he lets discharge inside his nice yellow covers.

I like your new poem, very much as the Toothy Beth (what happy little jingles you could write about a Toothy Beth) would like it. I like it, but can't say much more about it. There is usually some phrase, or simile, or line, or even stanza to which I object, or in which I find sometimes a purposely rough image I imagine to be unsuccessful because it is not smooth enough & sometimes a little gush-bubble that a rude snarl of mine can prick to nothing & sometimes a precious word (a 'burgeon' or a 'pinguid') which revolts against my waxy ear and my urny taste. But, in 'Sarcophagus', I can find nothing except a desire to be liked. And I fall to desire, as always, liking it with a toothed inarticulateness. It's a bit harmless, a little bit thin, I think.

I see no vast reason why it should have been written. But written it is, and read it have been, and like it I do. I'm not usually as dumb as this over a poem of yours. But, really, I've nothing at all to say about it. It's there, just there, and I like it. For which brilliant piece of criticism I shall be awarded the Neuburg biscuit – a weekly prize for the longest nothing in the vaguest words.

H. Corby seems a dirty boy. But you're too old a bird to be stoned by him. I think I should like to quarrel with H. Corby about the Justification of The Phallus In Architecture, or The Influence of Sodomy On Wickerwork. What a perverted time we boys would have.

Is, by the way, the Babs of the skyblue jumper the same Babs Ross who sometimes decorates the Poet's Corner with her sweet little name? Anybody who can write a poem & put Babs under it deserves a pat on the back. I lift my hat. Three moths and a woodpigeon, one calling your name, fly out. Ach, it is always the same. These woodpigeons . . .!

And now, before I get any archer, & start to crack very weak jokes about plums, let me go out for my much-talked of walk. Goodbye till tonight, my dear.

Morning. Sunday 13.

But the night never comes. And two loose days have passed since I wrote those last ink words. They were loose days, and I accept the reprimand – before it comes – with a bowed head and a dim, canary mouth. I don't know why I do it. It's silly and childish, but somehow inevitable, especially on a sunny Saturday evening in a seaside village where, most of the afternoon, I had laid in the sun, trying to colour my face and look out-of-doors.

I hate the little, minor disturbances of the world – the forgetting of letters, the losing of papers, the tiny falls, mishaps & disappointments which crop up, regular as the suicidal wish, each gassy day. Late night, in the deserted smokeroom of a seaside pub, I found myself suddenly cornered by three repulsive looking young men with coloured shirts, who asked me, in a most polite & Turpin way, for my cigarettes. Since they all looked *exactly* like Wallace Beery in one of his less debonair moments, I gave them my cigarettes and enough money to buy three pints of beer. They then smiled – or rather showed me about ten (or less) broken teeth (between them) – and persisted in drinking their illgotten beer in front of me & making rude remarks about the length of my hair. Now, I don't mind their communist ideas, or even the practice of them. But why *my* cigarettes, *my* beer, & *my* funny hair? It's little incidents like that that make one feel very weak & small in a country full of strong barbarians. Before they left me – probably to intimidate another lonely little person – they told me what was apparently a dirty story in Welsh. That was the last straw, & later the sun went out.

This morning, looking at Vicky's noncommittal remarks about Dylan Thomas, the experimentalist, I found myself wondering who this sad-named poet was, & whether he had any separate existence from the sadder person, of the night before, bullied out of his lawful cigarettes by three strongmen & falling back, in the event of his comic cowardice, on to a stony pile of words. And why should this experimentalist be given so many lines in a national newspaper, & my Beery-mouthed desperadoes be consigned to the mortality of a letter page?

Anyway, I'm not an experimentalist & never will be. I write in the only way I can write, & my warped, crabbed & cabinned stuff is not the result of theorising but of pure incapability to express my needless tortuities in any other way. Vicky's article was nonsense. If you see him, tell him I am not modest, not experimental, do not write of the Present, and have very little command of rhythm. My Pegasus, too, is much, much more spavined than that of A. L. Basham, who is too selfconscious, or Pamela Johnson, whose latest published 'Poem' is sweet, girlish drivel.

Tell him, too, that I don't know anything about life-rhythm. Tell him I write of worms and corruption, because I like worms and corruption. Tell him I believe in the fundamental wickedness and worthlessness of man, & in the rot in life. Tell him I am all for cancers. And tell him, too, that I loathe poetry. I'd prefer to be an anatomist or the keeper of a morgue any day. Tell him I live exclusively on toenails and tumours. I sleep in a coffin too, and a wormy shroud is my summer suit.

> 'I dreamed the genesis of mildew John
> Who struggled from his spiders in the grave'

is the opening of my new poem. So there. But I don't like words either. I like things like 'ungum' & 'casabookch'. XXX, for you, my bleeder.

All of which, I think, must be owing to the condition of the liver. But never forget that the heart took the liver's place.

My novel, tentatively, very tentatively, titled 'A Doom On The Sun' is progressing, three chapters of it already completed. So far it is rather terrible, a kind of warped fable in which Lust, Greed, Cruelty, Spite etc., appear all the time as old gentlemen in the background of the story. I wrote a little bit of it early this morning – a charming incident in which Mr Stipe, Mr Edger, Mr Stull, Mr Thade and Mr Strich watch a dog dying of poison. I'm a nice little soul, and my book is going to be as nice as me.

New story about Mae West: Mae West visited a farm while on a tour through the West States, & was taken around the farm by a handsome young farmhand. They came across a bull making love to a cow. 'Tell me,' said Mae West, 'How does the bull know exactly when the cow is – sort of – wanting to be made love to?' 'Waal,' sd the farmhand, 'It's all a matter of smell with these here animals.' Later they came across a ram and a ewe, also in a Lawrencian attitude. And on asking the same question,

Mae West received the same answer. As the farmhand saw her to her car, she turned round & said: 'This has been a real swell day. Say, you must come up and see me sometime – when your catarrh's better.'

Which leads me, quite naturally, to the end of this ridiculous letter. [*Some words are deleted.*] (Sorry. Had to cross this out. It was indecent.) I love you, Pamela, more every day, think of you more every day, and want to be with you more every day. Don't take much notice of my rantings and rumblings, and less of that horrid poem I sent you last week. I love you and love you. I only believe in you. Nice, round Pamela, I love you. All the time. Always will, too. Write very soon and keep me alive. Sorry for all my letter. I'm not too well – perhaps it's that. You don't mind how daft the letter, do you? If it's the mask I know, never lift it, my twiceblessed. Love, & the crosses I can't write because there's not room enough. P.S. What do you want for your birthday? Books? Rings? Wurlitzer Organ?

And now goodbye. I seem to be getting back into my old letter mood, and don't really want to stop writing. But I have to stop sometime, and I've already delayed this letter longer than I wanted to. Reply in a very few days, will you. And do be honest. Remember, I'm very fond of birds (Damn, that again!). Yes, do write back soon. Wave your hand to your mother for me, and kiss yourself goodmorning and goodnight.

Dylan

May, 1934 — Laugharne

I am spending Whitsun in the strangest town in Wales. Laugharne, with a population of four hundred, has a townhall, a castle, and a portreeve. The people speak with a broad English accent, although on all sides they are surrounded by hundreds of miles of Welsh county. The neutral sea lies at the foot of the town, and Richard Hughes writes his cosmopolitan stories in the castle.

I am staying with Glyn Gower Jones. You remember I showed you one of his bad poems in the Adelphi. He is a nice, handsome young man with no vices. He neither smokes, drinks, nor whores. He looks very nastily at me down his aristocratic nose if I have more than one Guinness at lunch, and is very suspicious when I go out by myself. I believe he thinks that I sit on Mr Hughes' castle walls with a bottle of rye whiskey, or revel in the sweet confusion of a broadflanked fisherwoman.

Incidentally, I showed him some of your poems, your latest poems. And he couldn't understand them at all. An ardent admirer of the Criterion, he fails to understand you. And it's quite true. You are getting pleasantly obscure, and much of what you write at the moment must seem quite mazy and difficult to almost anyone except myself. But then the reason is obvious. I, too, am mazy and difficult. We both are in our fleshly lives. And let me remind you that you will find my body damnably difficult to dispose of. 'That particular one' (your Bluebeard words) has found a widow. I will never find anyone except you. The only solution will be a little poison in my cup. Even then there would be the phantom Thomas, head under arm, three mackintoshed, weakchinned and blowsy, seeking you out and groaning his disembodied bawderies in your ear. Or, of course, you could garotte me as I nibble at my vermicelli.

(Rose plot,
Fringed pool,
Ferned garotte.)

I seem always to be complaining that I cannot fit the mood of my letters into the mood of the weathered world that surrounds me. Today I complain again, for a hell-mouthed mist is blowing over the Laugharne ferry, and the clouds lie over the chiming sky – what a conceit – like the dustsheets over a piano. Let me, O oracle in the lead of a pencil, drop this customary clowning, and sprinkle some sweetheart words over the paper, (paper torn slyly from an exercise book of the landlady's small daughter). Wishes, always wishes. Never a fulfilment of action, flesh. The consummation of dreams is a poor substitute for the breathlessness at the end of the proper windy gallop, bedriding, musical flight into the Welsh heavens after a little, discordant brooding over the national dungtip.

My novel of the Jarvis valley is slower than ever. I have already scrapped two chapters of it. It is as ambitious as the Divine Comedy, with a chorus of deadly sins, anagrammatised as old gentlemen, for the incarnated figures of Love & Death, an Ulyssean page of thought for the minds of the two anagrammatical spinsters, Miss P. & Miss R. Sion-Rees, an Immaculate Conception, a baldheaded girl, a celestial tramp, a mock Christ, & the Holy Ghost.

I am a Symbol Simon. My book will be full of footlights & Stylites, & puns as bad as that. Kiss me Hardy? Dewy love me? Tranter body ask? I'll Laugharne this bloody place for being wet. I'll pun so frequently and so ferociously that the rain will spring backward on an ambiguous impulse, & the sun leap out to light the cracks of this saw world.

But I won't tell you my puns, for they run over reason, and I want you to think of me today not as a bewildered little boy writing an idiot letter on the muddy edge of a ferry, watching the birds & wondering which among them is the 'sinister necked' wild duck & which the 'terrible' cormorant, but as a strong-shouldered fellow polluting the air with the smell of his eightpenny tobacco and his Harris tweeds, striding, golf-footed, over the hills and singing as loudly as Beachcomber in a world rid of Prodnose. There he goes, that imaginary figure, over the blowing mountain where the goats all look like Ramsay MacDonald, down the crags and the rat-hiding holes in the sides of the hill, on to the mud flats that go on for miles in the direction of the sea. There he stops for a loud & jocular pint, tickles the serving wench where serving wenches are always tickled, laughs with the landlord at the boatman's wit, ('The wind he be a rare one he be. He blows up the petticoats of they visiting ladies for the likes of we. And a rare thirst he give you. Pray fill the flowing bowl, landlord, with another many magnums of your delectable liquor. Aye, aye, zor'. And so on), and hurries on, still singing, into the mouth of the coming darkness. Or he hies him manfully to the Hikers' Hostel, removes his pimples with a bread knife, and sprinkles a little iodine over the one and forty bats that ring the changes in the Hikers' belfries.

But the eye of truth, tired of romancing, turns back with a material squint on my self, and marks the torture in my too-bony hand and the electric livingness in the bodies of the goldfish I carry in the lining of my hat. Pamela, never trust the goldfish in the lining. They dribble lead over the nice, new felt. And their molten excreta drops, with the noise of the drums in Berlioz, on to the open skull.

I am tortured to-day by every doubt and misgiving that an hereditarily twisted imagination, an hereditary thirst and a commercial quenching, a craving for a body not my own, a chequered education and too much egocentric poetry, and a wild, wet day in a tided town, are capable of conjuring up out of their helly deeps. Helly deeps. There is torture in words, torture in their linking & spelling, in the snail of their course on stolen paper, in their wound that the four winds double, and in my knowledge of their inadequacy. With a priggish weight on the end, the sentence falls. All sentences fall when the weight of the mind is distributed unevenly along the holy consonants & vowels. In the beginning was a word I can't spell, not a reversed Dog, or a physical light, but a word as long as Glastonbury and as short as pith. Nor does it lisp like the last word, break wind like Balzac through a calligraphied window, but speaks out sharp & everlasting with the intonations of death and doom on the magnificent syllables. I wonder whether I love your word, the word of your hair, – by loving hair I reject all Oscardom, for homosexuality is as bald as a coot –, the word of your voice, the word of your flesh, & the word of your presence. However good, I can never love you as earth. The good earth of your blood is always there, under the skin I love, but it is two words. There must be only half a word tangible, audible, & visible to the illiterate. And is that the better half? Or is it the wholly ghostly part? And does the oneeyed ferryman, who cannot read a printed word, row over a river of words, where the syllables of the fish dart out & are caught on his rhyming hook, or feel himself a total ghost in a world that's as matter-of-fact as a stone? If these were the only questions, I could be happy, for they are answered quickly with a twisting of sense into the old metaphysics. But there are other and more dreadful questions I am frightened to answer.

I am whimsy enough today to imagine that the oyster-catchers flying over the pearlless mudbanks are questioning all the time. I know the question and the answer, but I'm going to tell you neither, for it would make you sad to know how easily the answer drops off the tip of the brain. Fill up the pan of the skull with millet seed. Each seed shall be a grain of truth, & the mating grains pop forth an answer. (Bugger me black.)

I wish I could describe what I am looking on. But no words could tell you what a *hopeless*, fallen angel of a day it is. In the very far distance, near the line of the sky, three women & a man are gathering cockles. The oystercatchers are protesting in hundreds around them. Quite near me, too, a crowd of silent women are scraping the damp, gray sand with the torn-off handles of jugs, & cleaning the cockles in the drab little pools of water that stare up out the weeds & long for the sun. But you see that I am making it a literary day again. I can never do justice [*words deleted*] to the miles and miles and miles of mud and gray sand, to the un-nerving silence of the fisherwomen, & the mean-souled cries of the gulls & the herons, to the shapes of the fisherwomen's breasts that drop, big as barrels, over the stained tops of their overalls as they bend over the sand, to the cows in the fields that lie north of the sea, and to the near breaking of the heart as the sun comes out for a minute from its cloud & lights up the raggèd sails of a fisherman's boat. These things look ordinary enough on paper. One sees them as shapeless, literary things, & the sea is a sea of words, and the little fishing boat lies still on a tenth rate canvas. I can't give actuality to these things. Yet they are as alive as I. Each muscle in the cocklers' legs is as big as a hill, and each crude footstep in the wretchedly tinted sand is deep as hell. These women are sweating the oil of life out of the pores of their stupid bodies, and sweating away what brains they had so that their children might eat, be married and ravished, conceive in their wombs that are stamped with the herring, &, themselves, bring up another race of thickhipped fools to sweat their strength away on these *unutterably* deadly sands.

But now a piece of sun comes out again. I am happy, or, at least, free from this morning's tortures. Glyn has gone fishing, and in another half hour the 'Three Mariners' will have undone their waistcoats. I shall drink beer with the portreeve, & no crimping pussyfoot shall say me nay.

I forgot to bring your letter with me. It lies locked at home in the Pamela drawer. Its memory makes Laugharne a bit brighter – but still not bright enough – and it closed with the only words that should ever close a letter. But I can't remember many of its details. I'll reply to them again, or perhaps they can wait till I see you again. I shall look out for your tail-less story. I forgot to bring 'Anna' too. It is the best story you have written. You are becoming very competent, dear, and your stories are all your own. There are many things for me to say about 'Anna', but they, too, must wait.

Oh hell to the wind as it blows these pages about. I have no Rimbaud for a book or paper rest, but only a neat, brown rock upon which I have drawn three very ferocious travesties of your face – one eyeless, one toothless, & all entirely bloodless. Oh hell to the wind as it blows my hair over my forehead. And woe on the sun that he bloody well shines not.

Soon I see you. Soon I kiss you hullo.

It's getting cold, too cold to write. I haven't got a vest on, and the wind is blowing around the Bristol Channel. I agree with Buddha that the essence of life is evil. Apart from not being born at all, it is best to die young. I agree with Schopenhauer (he, in his philosophic dust, would turn with pleasure at my agreement) that life has no pattern & no purpose, but that a twisted vein of evil, like the poison in a drinker's glass, coils up from the pit to the top of the hemlocked world. Or at least I might do. But some things there are that are better than others. The tiny, scarlet ants that crawl from the holes in the rock on to my busy hand. The shapes of the rocks, carved in chaos by a tiddly sea. The three broken masts, like three nails in the breast of a wooden Messiah, that stick up in the far distance from a stranded ship. The voice of a snotty-nostrilled child sitting in a pool and putting shellfish in her drawers. The hundreds and hundreds of rabbits I saw last night as I lay, incorrigibly romantic, in a field of buttercups, & wrote of death. The jawbone of a sheep that I wish would fit into my pocket. The tiny lives that go slowly & liquidly on in the cold pools near my hands. The brown worms in beer. All these, like Rupert Brooke, I love because they remind me of you. Yes, even the red ants, the dead jawbone, & the hapless chemical. Even the rabbits, buttercups, & nailing masts.

Soon I see you. Write by the end of this week. Darling, I love you.

XXXX

27 May, 1934 in Bed

Question One. I can't come up
Two. I'm sleeping no better
Question Three. 'No' I've done everything that's wrong
Four. I daren't see the doctor
Question 5. Yes I love you

I'm in a dreadful mess now. I can hardly hold the pencil or see the paper. This has been coming for weeks. And the last four days have completed it. I'm absolutely at the point of breaking now. You remember how I was when I said goodbye to you for the first time. In the Kardomah when I loved you so much and was too shy to tell you. Well imagine me one hundred times worse than that with my nerves oh darling absolutely at the point of breaking in little bits. I can't think and I don't know what I'm doing When I speak I don't know if I'm shouting or whispering and that's a terrible sign. It's *all* nerves & no more But I've never imagined anything as bad.

And it's all my own fault too. As well as I can I'll tell you the honest, honest truth. I never want to lie to you. You'll be terribly angry with me I know and you'll never write to me again perhaps But darling you want me to tell you the truth don't you

I left Laugharne on Wednesday morning and went down to a bungalow in Gower. I drank a lot in Laugharne & was feeling a bit funny even then. I stayed in Gower with Cliff, who was a friend of mine in the waster days of the reporter's office. On Wednesday evening Billie his fiancée came down. She was tall & thin and dark with a loose red mouth & a harsh sort of laugh. Later we all went out & got drunk. She tried to make love to me all the way home. I told her to shut up because she was drunk When we got back she still tried to make love to me wildly like an idiot in front of Cliff. She went to bed and Cliff and I drank some more and then very modernly he decided to go & sleep with her. But as soon as he got in bed with her she screamed & ran into mine.

I slept with her that night & for the next three nights We were terribly drunk day & night Now I can see all sorts of things. I think I've got them.

Oh darling, it hurts me to tell you this but I've got to tell you because I always want to tell you the truth about me. And I never want to share It's you & me or nobody, you & me & nobody. But I've been a bloody fool & I'm going to bed for a week I'm just on the borders of DTs darling, and I've wasted some of my tremendous love for you on a lank redmouthed girl with a reputation like a hell. I don't love her a bit I love you Pamela always & always But she's a pain on the nerves. For Christ knows why she loves me Yesterday morning she gave her ring back to Cliff.

I've got to put a 100 miles between her & me

I must leave Wales forever & never see her

I see bits of you in her all the time & tack on to those bits I've got to be drunk to tack on to them

I love you Pamela & *must have* you As soon as all this is over I'm coming straight up. If you'll let me. No, but better or worse I'll come up next week if you'll have me. Don't be too cross or too angry What the hell am I to do? And what the hell are you going to say to me? Darling I love you & think of you all the time. Write by return And don't break my heart by telling me I mustn't come up to London to you becos I'm such a bloody fool. XXXX Darling. Oh Darling.

December, 1935

Hullo Pam,

I haven't written to you for such a long time that I'm tired of waiting for your reply; and neither has mother, catering for her invalids, including Arthur now, the pleasant uncle, answered your nice letter to her, and dad only answers bills. What a family. We all have our little aches, we moan, we plug ourselves with patent medicines. Dad has a new pain (isn't this lovely ink, it's called Quink) in the eye, mother has indigestion, Arthur has rheumatism and a cold, I cough. When *you* wrote last you were dying, almost cuddling the long, black guardian worm who is the exclusive death-property of the Johnsons. Are you better, my rose, my own? And you aren't cross with me? No, of course you aren't, my mole, my badger, my little blood-brown Eve. (That's how I feel.) But this is a shoddy letter and I'm not going to finish it – just to spite myself. I haven't written a word – except for incompetent thriller reviews – since I came home. Not even a letter. I feel too weak and too tired.

But here's a true story: Tom Warner is learning shorthand. On Monday he wrote the word 'egg' all day. On Tuesday he wrote the word 'kick' all day. On Wednesday he decided to revise Monday's work, sat down, and wrote 'eck'.

Tom plays the piano for Heather on Friday nights. It's driving him mad. He has to play Ketèlbey and Irving Berlin and selections from talkies.

It's no good. I can't write. I shall put this in an envelope and then sit looking at the fire. I love you. I am a blue-green buzzard and my name is Dylan.

WYN HENDERSON

Wyn Henderson, to whom the following letter is directed, was a woman in her late thirties with a weakness for artists when Dylan became involved with her in the spring of 1936. She had invited him to come stay for a while at her home in Porthcurno, Cornwall. Dylan went. Although the affair ended when Dylan met and fell in love with his future wife, he and Wyn remained on good terms.

March 9, 1936 5 Cwmdonkin Drive Uplands Swansea

Darling (Dylan) Darling (Dylan again) Wyn, and Oswell (if he's about),

How nice of you to purr about me after dinner, two fed, sleek cats rubbing against the table legs and thinking about a scrubby Welshman, with a three-weeks-accumulated hangover and a heart full of love and nerves full of alcohol, moping over his papers in a mortgaged villa in an upper-class professional row (next to the coroner's house) facing another row (less upper) and a dis-used tennis court. It was a lovely rolling letter, out of the depths of dinner, and a winy mantle of love hung over it, and thank you a lot, Wyn and Oswell.

Wyn privately: As your mascot and very welcome guest, I'd love to come to Cornwall more than anything else: it sounds just what I want it to be, and I can write poems, and stories about vampire sextons deflowering their daughters with very tiny scythes, and draw rude little pictures of three-balled clergymen, and go [to] pubs and walks with you. It's all too lovely to be good; and I'd enjoy it so much. I'm coming to town in about a fortnight: I've got to meet a few publishers and try to get money from them as I haven't any, and, I believe, to read some poems over the wireless. That won't take long: the publishers will (probably) pretend to be deaf, and the wireless will break down. If you are gone by then, chugging into Cornwall, shall I follow you and will you meet me, me lost, me with beer in my belly and straws in my hair? And if you haven't chugged away, but are still rampaging in Bloomsbury (or wherever you rampage mostly) we can go together, can't we? And that will be nicer still. (This letter, Wyn dear, is too excellently phrased. But I've just finished writing a story called The Phosphorescent Nephew; and whatever I do now, bugger me it's literary.)

So thanks, Wyn, for the invitation. I do hope you won't be gone when I come back to London – even though you have to go away and leave me there temporarily – because there are lots of little things to talk about.

Much love to you, (and to old Slime, the State Parasite).

Dylan

CAITLIN MACNAMARA

Caitlin Macnamara met Dylan Thomas in a pub in London early in 1936. He was 21 and she ten months older. Legend has it they were introduced by the painter Augustus John, who had been and probably still was Caitlin's lover. The story goes that the two men fought over Caitlin, a circumstance that would have caused the free-spirited part French part Irish dancer very little anguish. Dylan and Caitlin married in July 1937, the marriage licence paid for by Wyn Henderson. Their marriage was famously tempestuous, and sometimes violent, and was close to breaking point when Dylan left for his last trip to the USA. Despite the tempests, they clung to each other like shipwrecked orphans through years of poverty, excess and success. They had three children together: Llewelyn, Aeronwy and Colum.

July 17, 1936 5 Cwmdonkin Drive Uplands Swansea

Caitlin darling darling, I caught lots of buses and went to sleep in them and ate wine gums in the train and got here awfully late in a sort of thunder storm. This morning I can't do anything but sit with my headache and my liver in a higgledy piggledy room looking out on the rain, and now I'm trying to keep my hand steady to write a neat letter to you that isn't all miserable because I'm not with you in Laugharne or in London or in Ringwood or whatever daft place you're in without me. I dreamed all sorts of funny dreams in my big respectable feather bed – which is much much better than a battlement bed full of spiders – dreams with you in them all the time, and terrible ticking clocks, and vampires, and ladies with long arms putting out the light, and intimate black dogs just sitting on us. I love you Caitlin. I love you more than anybody in the world. And yesterday – though it may be lots of yesterdays ago to you when this wobbly letter reaches you – was the best day in the world, in spite of dogs, and Augustus woofing, and being miserable because it had to stop. I love you for millions and millions of things, clocks and vampires and dirty nails and squiggly paintings and lovely hair and being dizzy and falling dreams. I want you to be with me; you can have all the spaces between the houses, and I can have a room with no windows; we'll make a halfway house; you can teach me to walk in the air and I'll teach you to make nice noises on the piano without any music; we'll have a bed in a bar, as we said we would, and we shan't have any money at all and we'll live on other people's, which they won't like a bit. The room's full of they now, but I don't care, I don't care for anybody. I want to be with you because I love you.

I don't know what I love you means, except that I do. [*words deleted*] (I crossed that out. It was, 'In 21 messy years', but I don't know what I was going to say). Write to me soon, very very soon, and tell me you really mean the things you said about you loving me too; if you don't I shall cut my throat or go to the pictures.

I'm here in a nest of schoolmasters and vicars, majors, lawyers, doctors, maiden aunts; and you're lord knows where, in the country, miles and miles from me, painting barmy ivy. Now I'm sad, I'm sad as hell, and I'll have to go to a pub by myself & sit in the corner and mope. I'm going to mope about you and then I'm going to have a bath and I'm going to mope about you in the bath. Damn all this anyway; I only want to tell you all the time and over & over again that I love you and that I'm sad because you've gone away and that I'm not going to lose you and that I'm going to see you soon and that I want us to get married once we can and that you said yes you wanted to too. And write to me when you get this, or before you do, only write and tell me all there is to tell me. And I'll write to tell you when I'll be in London, and then we'll meet, however much they try to stop us, and then I'll be happy again and I'll try to make you happy by not being a half wit. All my love for as long as forever & ever is Dylan

XX

November or December 1936

Nice, lovely, faraway Caitlin my darling,

Are you better, and please God you aren't too miserable in the horrible hospital? Tell me everything, when you'll be out again, where you'll be at Christmas, and that you think of me and love me. And when you're in the world again, we'll both be useful if you like, trot round, do things, compromise with the They people, find a place with a bath and no bugs in Bloomsbury, and be happy there. It's that – the *thought* of the few, simple things we want and the *knowledge* that we're going to get them in spite of you know Who and His spites and tempers – that keeps us living I think. It keeps *me* living. I don't want you for a day (though I'd sell my toes to see you now my dear, only for a minute, to kiss you once, and make a funny face at you): a day is the length of a gnat's life: I want you for the lifetime of a big, mad animal, like an elephant. I've been indoors all this week, with a wicked cold, coughing and snivelling, too full of phlegm and aspirins to write to a girl in hospital, because my letter would be sad and despairing, & even the ink would carry sadness & influenza. Should I make you sad, darling, when you're in bed with rice pudding in Marlborough Ward? I want so very much to look at you again; I love you; you're weeks older now; is your hair grey? have you put your hair up, and do you look like a real adult person, not at all anymore beautiful and barmy like the proper daughters of God? You mustn't look too grown-up, because you'd look older than me; and you'll never, I'll never let you, grow wise, and I'll never, you shall never let me, grow wise, and we'll always be young and unwise together. There is, I suppose, in the eyes of the They, a sort of sweet madness about you and me, a sort of mad bewilderment and astonishment oblivious to the Nasties and the Meanies; you're the only person, of course you're the only person from here to Aldebaran and back, with whom I'm free entirely; and I think it's because you're as innocent as me. Oh I know we're not saints or virgins or lunatics; we know all the lust and lavatory jokes, and most of the dirty people; we can catch buses and count our change and cross the roads and talk real sentences. But our innocence goes awfully deep, and our discreditable secret is that we don't know anything at all, and our horrid *inner* secret is that we don't care that we don't. I've just read an Irish book called Rory and Bran, and it's a bad charming book: innocent Rory falls in love with innocent Oriana, and, though they're both whimsy and talk about the secret of the language of the hills and though Rory worships the moon and Oriana glides about in her garden listening to the legendary birds, they're not as mad as we are, nor as innocent. I love you so much I'll never be able to tell you; I'm frightened to tell you. I can always feel your heart. Dance tunes are always right: I love you body and soul: – and I suppose body means that I want to touch you & be in bed with you, & I suppose soul means that I can hear you & see you & love you in every single, single thing in the whole world asleep or awake.

Dylan X

I wanted this to be a letter full of news, but there isn't any yet. It's just a letter full of what I think about you and me. You're not empty, empty still now, are you? Have you got love to send me?

EMILY HOLMES COLEMAN

Emily Holmes Coleman was an American writer based in London. She was the author of one novel, the autobiographical The Shutters of Snow *(1930). She was fourteen years older than Dylan, which may have added to her attractions. They became involved after Dylan had met Caitlin, and their romance blossomed while Caitlin was away in Ireland and Dylan alone in London.*

January 28 & 29, 1937 Cwmdonkin Drive Uplands
Swansea

darling Emily dear, dear Emily darling, Emily Emily dear Emily,

I think of you so much. I think of us, and all the funny, nice things we've done, and all the nicer things we're going to do. I think of nice places and people, and, when I think of them, you're always there, always tall and death-mouthed and big-eyed and no-voiced, with a collegiate ribbon or a phallic hat. I think of us in pubs and clubs and cinemas and beds. I think I love you.

What little beast told you I didn't leave on the Taffy train that night? I left, my God I left, and the train took seven hours instead of four, stopping at every single station while the guard told dirty stories to the stationmaster and naked porters danced among the milk-churns and the ticket-collector abused himself over his punching-machine and the driver buggered the fireman on the footplate. I didn't look out of the window, but I knew what was happening: I had psychic claustrophobia, and could tell by each reverberation and roar of the rails exactly what position the fireman was in. The train smelt of lust and armpits and lava-bread. I was home at half-past-eight in the morning, very weak, very vague, and I slept for two days. I grew very friendly, by the way, with the drunken man we found asleep: his name was Duck, he was fifty two years old, he had a son my age who was a commercial traveller, he himself was a coal-exporter and he said he had met Greta Garbo in Tunbridge Wells. I think he was a liar, but he was a nice man too and he invited me to stay with his family any time I liked. I'm not going to, though: I may see Wallace Beery in Gloucester. Mr Duck was a life-long subscriber to the Film Weekly, the Picturegoer, Film Fun, The Cinema Weekly, and the Film Gazette. He liked films.

What are you doing? Have you retired to your kitten and temple? I'm in my bowlerland again, hemmed in by vicars, but it's only to-day, just over a week since I left you, dear, that I've started to work. After two days' sleep I was like a little bull, a little spotty bull, and I endured without alcohol. Brainlessly, I cut out drink, and only my sane mother saved my sanity, driving me out to the pubs with a stern but sad demand to drink myself steady. Now I am fit again, though scabious, and my three pints a night – from nine-o'-clock until ten – are a legitimate heaven. This morning I started on a story that I dreamed about a blind horse and a wooden woman, and this evening, like a fallen cherub at my window facing the park, I'm writing to you, to Emily, to my darling, inaudible, scabious, American Emily. I love you.

Don't worry your head about Norman's venereal warning; he's timid and jealous. Shall I give you a lecture on Norman? Norman is good, but too much of him is made personally interesting and interestingly eccentric through financial invulnerability. His brusqueness and rudeness, even his intolerance of shams, wouldn't be half so effective – wouldn't, perhaps, be at all – if he weren't entirely immune from the attacks of money and the lack of it. He is able to maintain his literary honesty through the dishonesty of property, his social honesty through (to me) the unsociability of a private income. He will never have a real friend until he realises that; real friendship is built up on mutual need – need for everything, pooled love, pooled possessions, pooled lack of possessions, pooled contacts, pooled miseries – while all that Norman needs from a friend is friendship, and friendship, to him, is only acquaintanceship that has gone on for sufficiently long. He has so many friends because he can turn easily from one to another, asking little from each but companionship. He has never *tried* a friend's friendship to the full, is ignorant of the extent to which real friendship *can* be tried; and, therefore, when his own friendship is tried, it fails. It fails through his lack of experience: he can open his heart to let lots of people in, but he can't open it out altogether for one person: he covers his heart with half-friends to conceal its nakedness from the advances of a whole friend: he doesn't understand that a real friend is always naked, that a real friend doesn't have to undress but that he just has no clothes to wear in front of him. Norman understands nothing of the reasons that bind people together; from a man, 'Love thy neighbour' is, to him, homosexual; he can't understand that people are bound together because of what they *give out* to each other, not because of what they offer to each other: – (and a companion is always offering, offering anecdotes, intimacies, hospitalities, while a friend is giving out all the real, warm things that lie so very deep underneath all those material offerings). And he can't understand – just because he has, inside himself, had no experience of it – that, though a single little match can set the world on fire, altering its appearance, the things that made up that world, all the causes and forces and bases of the world, can never alter. I mean he understands people so little that, when their *appearances* alter under altering circumstances, he is confronted by them as by strangers. He looks for a rigid conformity in the hearts of his friends; even if he found it he would not know it, for he doesn't understand that the only conformity is that of Affection, that the heart moves but does not alter, that even when the heart has moved a universe away from him it remains, in what it originally *gave out*, unalterable for ever. A wind from anywhere can blow anything about willy-nilly, but any shape that anything once had is static; you can pull the moon down, but the moon always remains in exactly the same shape and position as when you saw it clearly for the first time. This is all frightfully clumsy, but it's true. It's something that old Norman must learn through himself; otherwise, he will suffer and die through an ingrowing heart.

What funny people we know. Antonia too. I've been thinking about her. I think Antonia will never recover from once having been mad. She was a tame cat in a cage who always, much against her waking will, was dreaming of liberty; and then, one waking day, obsessed by those dreams, she escaped into liberty, a liberty that for her – necessarily because of her long, tame imprisonment – was far more terrifying than the safety behind the suburban-zoo bars. So at last she crawled back to the zoo, through a million strange and frightening places full of human wild animals, and now she is done for, done for ever perhaps. She wants to be tame again, but she's been let loose once. Now tame companions are no good for her, and wild companions frighten her; the only companions she feels comfortable with now are those, like herself, who have been brought up tame and dream of a wild liberty, but those, at the same time, who have never got beyond dreaming of it and who therefore have few of her own fears. Mr Gascoyne, conscientiously pursuing his Richmond sanity right to the gates of the insane institutions, has always been too careful to try to unlock the gates: a poetical surrealist in a looney-bin is a literary freak, but a surrealist who hangs around outside, pimping through the bars at the looney-logical activities of the inmates, can always be a man-of-letters and an acknowledged authority on the dark bits of the brain. So Antonia is comfortable with him, because he is a tame animal striving very hard to enjoy his zealously cultivated half-liberty; she, poor dear, was a tame animal forced through dreams into an unwelcome liberty, and is now a wild animal wanting so very very hard to enjoy the lack of liberty which she welcomed. That's all clumsy too, and it's true too I think. I don't know Peggy at all, otherwise I'd give a speech about *her*. And Phyllis doesn't seem to me to be complicated at all: she's just a good guy.

I don't really know about Caitlin. I don't know how tough my Caitlin is, how powerful her vagueness is, whether the sweet oblivion in which she moves about is proof against the little tiny hurts that can eat through a mountain while the big hurts just batter against it. I know she hasn't got much feeling about *physical* pain: she once wanted to boil a lobster but hadn't got a saucepan big enough, so she found a small saucepan and boiled the thing bit by bit while it screamed like a frog or a baby and drove us howling out. I know she's done away with most of the natural sense of surprise; nothing, I think, can shock her except squeamishness, and she can blush like a naked schoolgirl too. Of course I shall sleep with her; she's bound up with me, just as you are; one day I shall marry her very much – (no money, quite drunk, no future, no faithfulness) – and that'll be a funny thing.

I've been writing most of this – this probably too moral nonsense – in my aunts' house in Carmarthen, where I often stay, and I came back this Thursday morning to find your little telegram letter waiting. I know, my dear dear, that I should have written before, but time, since London, has been such a humourless muddle of headaching days and lonely heartaching nights packed to the skull and ceiling with great, blind, fleshlike, over-familiar dreams that fight and destroy themselves in the dark; there doesn't seem to have been any regular succession of hours, and half-past-nine has followed midnight, and almost the moon has risen at midday. And I didn't want to write, either, until my brain was cool; I wanted a true, honest letter, not the hysterical hangover I should certainly have suffered on paper had I written before this. My hands still shake, but I know my head now: and my head says 'Hullo, Emily', and inquires after your health, and hopes you aren't too unhappy, and tells you I love you. I know my heart too, but that's dumb as a red egg and is silent even when it breaks (I'm told).

FRIDAY I'm finishing this on the floor of my bedroom in front of a gasfire on which water is boiling to make me some nourishing tea. It's been snowing all night and is still snowing: my very special field is quiet and padded, it looks like white rubber: I didn't know before that snow had such a rubbery kick: my field's a springboard, and the barmy birds who are searching for snow-worms are shot up and down in the air like ping-pong balls on a fountain. It's half past ten in the morning: are you asleep? I wish I was fast asleep by your side, very warm, dreaming about the milk-white birds of Eden and the blue goats of Gehenna; and I wish, (at this moment in time that will never be again until time stops and then works backwards from Resurrection to Genesis, the last Trumpet note to the first Word, from the darkness of Judgement to Light), that I was waking up by your side, turning round slowly to see your face in the first of the shining, snowy morning. I wish I was with you. Never care what people say, my darling: Peggy's 'He won't write', & Antonia's 'He doesn't love you' and Norman's 'Beware, beware!' I shall always write to you, and always love you, & never hurt you purposely: never hurt you at all, you're a very rare and expensive animal, and Christ knows I'm a lucky little man to love you & have you loving me. I'd write lots more, but my fingers are decomposing, and I must keep enough strength to shudder my way outside and give bread to the starlings. Will you write me a letter very soon, please? Tell me everything you want to tell me; tell me what you're doing and what you're thinking; tell me about boozy Bob and stallion D'arcy and red leg-opening Phyllis, and tidy Tony, and that intolerable pouf your cat. Tell me tell me tell me tell me...

And don't be cross that I've been so long writing.

Dylan

I'm coming back to town, only for a few days, about *February 14*, before going to Oxford to lecture; then I'm going home & coming up again about *March 4*, for a few days, before going to Cambridge to lecture. Shall I see you then? Let's do everything in the world – (though I know what we'll do, of course: just go to pubs and bed. And what could be lovelier, anyway? I'm always happy with you.)

Give my love to anybody you see. But keep most of it. (And don't give any to James Travers: it would be mental necrophily).

February 11, 1937 Swansea

Emily darling,

It's good that you write to me: I like your letters like whiskey and cherries and smoke and honey, and always I understand at least half of the handwriting. Now this is just a very short note to tell you things; I'm up to my eyes in lectures, and anyway all the things I could want to write to you I'll be telling you soon. I have to give two lectures to the Cambridge something-or-other on Saturday & Sunday (13th, I think, and 14th), and in order to arrive there with a clear tongue I shan't stop in London before; I'll go to Cambridge straight from here, and then return some time on Monday. I'll ring you immediately. We'll have a million celebration drinks, and cover the English night with a Welsh American glory. And yes: I got rid of my spots for 2 days, then they returned to me, crying out Daddy. So I'll have to start all over again, (with you), though my hands are like lilies now. Monday then. I've missed you terribly.

XX
Dylan

Easter Monday, March 29, 1937 'Marston' Bishopston
Glamorgan

Emily darling,

We've moved to a small house – lawn, miniature drive, garage and mortgage – in the country by the sea, five minutes' walk from the cliffs of Pwllddu and Brandy Cove; and the weather's blue and soft, with a fine chill wind to make edges; and old men plough up and down among the cabbages behind the house, and seagulls complain to the scarecrows, and sheep and cows and trippers leave manure and sandwiches regularly in the foreground of our well-mown view; and I can stretch my legs to the Joiners' Arms, and do a lyric straddling on a stile, and hear in the near distance the voices of the Valley girls cry rape and resignation. I would have written to you sooner had not my mother been so seriously ill; she still is ill, with acute neuralgia in the roots of the nerves of her face, is weak as a moth, can't move at all in bed, and worries the daylight out of the window. I loved your wire and letter; remember me very much to Phyllis Jones: has she met the map of Ireland yet? she deserves the nicest man in London, all for herself; and would he appreciate that lovely, lean favourite? I have made some new old friends; I am, if you read Dickens, Dylan Veneering. The only democratic conception of human equality is that all men are tragic and comic: we die; we have noses. We are not united by our drabness and smallness, but by our heroisms; the common things are wonderful; the drab things are those that are not common. And I am inequal to a woman (for an unnecessary example) only in the sense that I am not so womanly. It's only among poor failures that I find the people I like best: the rich can, as a generalisation, achieve originality only by becoming a little insane. Cyril Connolly (an example chosen for no reason I can think of) is small because he has continually to be *proving*; the great character is his own proof of everything: he is not successful, because he is too busy: the glory of the world is narrow: he is too big for it. And it's the grossness of folly I love. (I love you too, but that's a happening, not, I think, a basis for events as is my love for Mr Fork, the crippled woodwork master, Mr Plane, the darting waiter, Mr Dish, the drunken clerk, the ham actor, the faded beauty, the assistant assistant film-producer.) It's a Welsh bank-holiday, a very social day, and soon I shall join the cold picnic-parties on the cliffs, drink beer in the 'bus-depôt, find a tripper's knicker in the gully, be a pocket Chesterton on the rolling, inn-roads. Of all days I like these crowded days the best; I'm sitting at the window, not to miss a motor or a tandem or a hiking shop-assistant, not to miss one shout or backfire, one squabbling little boy, one lanky schoolgirl full of candles and tomorrow, one yesterday's market-gardener remembering the Easter fairs at Neath and Oystermouth before the great West died. And on Thursday I'm going to North Wales with a haversack and a flapped cap.

My only news is nonsense. If you can get to a wireless, try to listen to the Western Region on the twenty first of April: I'm reading some poems: Auden's Ballad, John Short's Carol, one of my own. Caitlin has knitted me a sweater out of raw brown sheeps' wool, and I look like a London shepherd in 1890. Fred Janes is painting the portrait of a lump of paper. My story about the burning of the sea is smouldering on: 'There was a sore procession driven down the waters of the Bristol Channel, loud-toothed and tailed, with a sharp trumpet full of fishes and an emerald, soaked drum, towards the high cliff on which she stood that afternoon before the misadventures that befell the sea and country, the first catastrophe, the blinding of the horse and the self-destruction of the dead, the flight of the woodpeckers and the burning of all the navigable world'. There's hardly anything to say; I miss you deeply, and want to come back to London soon; I remember everything, and it's all good to remember. You are very, very near to me.

Now I'm going out to make or break my social links with the bright, chapped Easter world.

Love to you my dear, now & always,

Dylan

I'll write a longer letter on my daft Journey, full of facts and dreams and lectures and little drawings.

CAITLIN MACNAMARA

May, 1937 59 Gt. Ormond St W1

Caitlin Caitlin my love I love you, I can't tell you how much, I miss you until it hurts me terribly. Can you come up to London before I go to Wales again, because I think I shall have to be in Wales a long time, a couple of months almost; I've been in a nursing home with bronchitis and laryngitis or something, no voice at all, no will, all weakness and croaking and spitting and feeling hot and then feeling cold, and I'm about now but quavery and convalescent and I must see you. I haven't seen or written to you or let you know I'm alive – which, at the moment, and remembering neurasthenically my days of almost-death, I don't think I was – since Wednesday, the 21st of April, when I lost you in the morning, found money, and shouted on the wireless. Darling, you mustn't have been angry with me for not writing my love, my love which can't ever move but is growing always; you must not have disbelieved, for one little split hair of the day or night, that day and night I think of you, love you, remember everything all the time, and know forever that we'll be together again – & Christ knows where – because it must be like that. But I don't want to write words words words to you: I must see you and hear you; it's hell writing to you now: it's lifting you up, (though I'm sure I'm not strong enough), and thinking you are really my flesh-&-blood Caitlin whom I love more than anyone has loved anyone else, & then finding a wooden Caitlin like a doll or a long thin Caitlin like a fountain pen or a mummy Caitlin made before the bible, very old and blowable-away. I want you. When you're away from me, it's absolutely a physical removal, insupportable & irreparable: no, not irreparable: if I lost a hand when you weren't with me, when you came back it would grow again, stronger & longer than ever. That's my cock words again, though all it means is true as heaven: that it's nonsense me living without you, you without me: the world is unbalanced unless, in the very centre of it, we little muts stand together all the time in a hairy, golden, more-or-less unintelligible haze of daftness. And that's more words, but I love and love you. Only love, and true love. Caitlin Caitlin this is unbearable. Will you forgive me again – for being ill and too willy-minded & weak and full of useless (no God, not useless) love for you, love that couldn't bear writing even if it could, to write & say, I'm dying perhaps, come & see me quickly, now, with some gooseberries and kisses for me. I'm not dying now, much. If you're where I'm writing to – please everything you are – can you telephone here? And come up? & be with me somewhere, if only for an only I don't know how long? Please, Caitlin my dear.

XXXXXX

Caitlin

Dylan X Caitlin

Dylan

I have to be abstemious.

RUTH WYNN OWEN

Ruth Wynn Owen was a young Welsh actress Dylan met in Bradford in 1942 when he was making a wartime documentary. Perhaps she fell in love with him, others did, but he was married, she was married and she had scruples.

May, 1942 as from 13 Hammersmith Tce W6

no, not any longer after Saturday.
So will you – if you will
write, please – please write
to the film address.

Your letter – thank you very, very much for it; I was terribly glad to hear – came just after I had been seeing you on the films, you with your wand, showing a ladderless leg in the wings. You looked, if I may or mayn't say so, pretty good to me, and I wish you were in London, where even the sun's grey and God how I hate it, and not in Preston with a lot of sillies. I do hate the life here, the grey gets in your eyes so that a bit of green nearly blinds you and the thought of the sea makes you giddy as you cross the road like a bloody beetle. You wrote to me on a moor, and I write to you in a ringing, clinging office with repressed women all around punishing typewriters, and queers in striped suits talking about 'cinema' and, just at this very moment, a man with a bloodhound's voice and his cheeks, I'm sure, full of Mars Bars, rehearsing out loud a radio talk on 'India and the Documentary Movement'. I wish I were on the Halifax moor talking to you, not to dishonest men with hangovers. Perhaps I shall be able to give a long-postponed talk to the Cambridge English Society during the week of June 8, which would be wonderful because perhaps you don't work all day and perhaps you would come out with me, walk somewhere, watch me drink a pint, and talk and talk and talk. Would you like that? If you would, then I could try very hard to come up for a day. Let me know will you?

You said you wrote a bad letter, and you wrote a lovely one, though too short. I said, horribly, that I wrote a good letter, and I'm almost inarticulate. What's a good letter anyway? To put down a bit of oneself to send to someone who misses it? To be funny and selfconscious or self-consciously formal, or so very natural that even the words blush and stammer? I only know I'd prefer to talk to you, but as I've got to write because you're a million miles away, in the mild and bitter north, then I must write anything, anything or everything, just as it comes into the thing that keeps my collar from vanishing into my hat. First, how very very odd it was, coming across you out of the blue, out of the black, out of the blue-and-black bruise of a smutty town at the end of a witless week, when everything had gone wrong, I had gone wrong, as I didn't know then, only to come extravagantly right. I saw, suddenly, a human being, rare as a Martian, an actual unaffected human being, after months and months, and years indeed of meeting only straw men, sponge and vanity boys, walking sacks full of solid vinegar and pride, all the menagerie of a world very rightly at war with itself. (And now even the ink is spitting.) I felt, at once, so at ease with you that I can still hardly believe it.

Thank you for saying about Llewelyn. He's going away, tomorrow, for a few weeks to his grandmother, quite near Salisbury. Just outside Fordingbridge. I have to move from Hammersmith Terrace, and am trying to get a house in St Peter's Square to share with some people who have furniture. You don't know, I suppose, anyone who has any furniture stored in London and who would want to give it a good home? The only things I have are a deckchair with a hole in it, half a dozen books, a few toys, and an old iron. These would not fill even a mouse's home. It is very good sometimes to have nothing; I want society, not me, to have places to sit in and beds to lie in; and who wants a hatstand of his very own? But sometimes, on raining, nostalgic Sunday afternoons, after eating the week's meat, it would, however cowardly, whatever a blanketing of responsibility and conscience, be good to sprawl back in one's own bourgeois chair, bought slippers on one's trotters. But to hell with it, I want to talk about you, I know too much about myself: I've woken up with myself for 28 years now, or very nearly. But I can't write about you – and now the spitting pen is broken and the ink over documents ostentatiously and falsely called Important – because, though I feel much, I know so little. So goodbye for a time, and the smaller the time the better – at least for me. You will write? And I will see you?

love,
Dylan

August 28, 1942 Talsarn Cardiganshire

Ruth my dear,

I missed you; and I think that I must have willed myself to miss you that night after the theatre; not of my thinking self, whatever that vain, paste and cotton-wool wad of my self may matter, for I tried hard to reach the Salisbury or the stagedoor; I think I must have willed my lateness and weakness, willed it because, simply, I was ashamed of my hysterical excitement of the wet-eyed and over-protesting night before. I remembered losing my head in Piccadilly, which left very little for my heart had gone two months ago, gone into your by-me-unkissed breast. And you'll have to forgive now, along with my tears, protestations, and denials, my almost archly over-writing writing in this late, loving letter. I can be natural – my behaviour, then, in the black streets was as natural as my too-much drink and my giddiness at seeing you again allowed me – but perhaps my nature itself is over-written and complicate me out of this, you Ruth in a well. Was there something a little clinical in your attitude, or was it my windy head that blew your words about and got me dancing with love and temper among the bloody buses? I'm sure, and this isn't a mock-modest wish to be stroked back into vanity, that you were all right and I was all wrong. I had time wrong, I was thrusting its hands, instead of letting it move passionately gently until we could in time's good time be as near as we wished and we must. So forgive me: I'll follow the ticking old fossil until it's the Now Now hour, I'll follow it through the provincial towns and sail with it under the stagey bridges.

Believe me, I love you too.

And when will you be back in London? I shall go back from Wales on Tuesday. Will you wire me? I think that is the best: everything that comes here is unopened except bottles. And if you don't, or forget to, I will phone the stagedoor. We must find each other again and when we meet again I'll be more controlled and, indeed, even sane.

The cocks are crowing in the middle of the afternoon, and the sun is frying.

Will you trust me?

It is grand and lovely to have known you for even a little for such a little time.

I hope you are well and I know you are sweet and more than sweet to *me*.

When we are together next, let it be on your whole free day or at least on your whole free evening. Time will not let me say or ask more than that.

Dylan

CAITLIN THOMAS

1943 8 Wentworth Studios SW3

Monday, in a misery in our leaking studio, among vermin and falling plaster & unwashed plates.

My Own Caitlin, my dear darling,

It's never been so useless and lonely away from you as it

is this time; there is nothing to live for without you, except for your return or when I can [come] down to Laugharne which must, somehow, be this week because I love you far more than ever and I will not exist without your love and loveliness, darling, so please write and tell me you miss me, too, and love me, and think of us being, soon, together for ever again. By the time you get this, you'll also have got, I hope, *a bit more money* which I will wire either tonight or tomorrow morning. I could not send any more on Friday as there were so many things to pay; & some rent, too.

There is *nothing* to do without you; so terribly terribly sad to come back to our empty barn, lie all night in our big bed, listening to the rain & our mice and the creaks & leaks and the warnings; so sad I could die if I hadn't got to see you again & live with you always & always, when I woke up without you, think of you hundreds of miles away with Aeronwy Lil at your breasts that I want to kiss because I love you, my Cat. I hope to God I can come down for 2 or 3 days at the end of the week.

Last night I called on pudding Vera who has been in bed for over a week with apathy and illusions and who said she'd written to you about Gelli. She did not know you were in Laugharne, & when I told her she said could she spend a week or a bit *in* Laugharne with you before going on *with* you to Gelli for a week or a bit? And I said I'd tell you, I knew nothing about it.

How is it in Laugharne? Tell me everything; and especially that you love me & want me as I love & want you now, at this moment, and for every moment of my life & yours always. How is Frances, Mrs Wood (?), & Ivy?

I have seen some, not too many, of the usual people: Dan. The Rat who has now sold everything in his den or hole except that double revolting bed. My office horrors. Nobody I want to see at all because there is only one person I ever want to see and that is you darling oh oh darling I love you I want to be with you.

I'm going to the Chelsea tonight. Alone. And then back to think about you in bed. Give my love to Aeronwy. Every bit of my love to you, every substance & shadow of it, every look & thought & word. Oh I hate it without you.

xxxxxxx
Dylan

PS I work in Elstree, have to leave Chelsea frightfully early. I hate Elstree & Chelsea, too; very much. I have seen one or two films, halfquarrelled again with J. Eldridge, & over-wound the clock which I shall take to a man.
PSS What do you want me to send you? Books? Shawls? Skirts? Napkins? Cloak? Shoes I see on the floor? I'll send money anyway, and, I hope to God, myself. Kiss me. I'll say your name *very loudly* tonight as I put out the light.
PSSS Are you going to go over to Blaen-Cwm again? I'll write to them tomorrow.
PSSSS No more, dear, until I send a few pounds.

OH DARLING. X

1943 King's Arms Stirling Corner Barnet Herts

Darling:
Darling:
Caitlin my dear dear Cat.

It's awful to write to you because, even though I love writing to you, it brings you so near me I could almost touch you and I know at the same time that I *cannot* touch you, you are so far away in cold, unkind Ringwood and I am in stale Barnet in a roadhouse pub with nothing but your absence and your distance, to keep my heart company.

I think of you always all the time. I kiss my uncharitable pillow for you in the nasty nights. I can see you with our little Mongolian monkey at your breast; I can see you in that unfond house listening with loathing to the News; I can see you in bed, more lovely than anything that has ever been at all. I love you. I love Llewelyn & Aeronwy, but you above all and forever until the sun stops and even after that.

And I cannot come down this weekend. I have to work all day Sunday. I am working, for the first time since I sold my immortal soul, very very hard, doing three months' work in a week. I hate film studios. I hate film workers. I hate films. There is nothing but glibly naive insecurity in this huge tinroofed box of tricks. I do not care a bugger about the Problems of Wartime Transport. All I know is that you are my wife, my lover, my joy, my Caitlin.

But Cat darling I miss you too much to bear.

Come Back on Wednesday. I'll send you another inarticulately loving letter tomorrow, with some money. You should have it by Saturday morning. No, it's better that I wire the money so that you can have it for the weekend. Even though I dislike Blashford very much, I envy it because all my love is there with my children and with you.

Come back on Wednesday. *Please.*

I haven't been in London at all as I have to start working unlikelily early in the morning & carry on until six o'clock.

I love you more, even, than when I said I loved you only a few seconds ago.

I think I can get Vera a little part in this film: a tiny part as a pudding-faced blonde sloth but I shan't tell her that.

Write to me telling me two things: that you love me & that you are coming back on Wednesday which is like a day full of birds & bells.

I am writing on the back of a script by Mr J. B. Priestley. But that doesn't spoil what I have to say to you. I have to say to you that I love you in life & after death, and that even though I drink I am good. I am not drinking much. I am too lonely even for that.

Write.

Give my love to the pigmy baby & kiss Llewelyn on the forehead for me.

Touch your own body for me, very gently. On the breast & the belly. My Caitlin.

Your
Dylan
X

RUTH WYNN OWEN

September 19, 1943 Carmarthenshire

Ruth, my Dear,

It's over a year, I think, or know, since I wrote to you with my heart on my sleeve; now the shape of the hidden heart is arrowed, bloody, with a children's on-a-tree inscription under it: X loves Y, though those aren't the names. I've been in Wales for some weeks now, and have had time and a rinsed head enough to be able to write what I want. In London, I mean to write you every day, but the laziness, the horror and selfpity, that London drizzles down on me, stop everything but the ghost of a hope that perhaps you will ring, will drop a postcard to say you have come to town and would like to see me, or, ghostliest of all the half-hopes, that you might turn the corner of a street I am walking and that all the traffic will stop and the sirens suddenly sing sweetly, At last! at last!

Not that I had any right to think that you might write me, ring me, meet me; it was my turn, but I was too cowardly to go on, thinking that you might tire or say, forever, go away and no more.

But I want to forget the falsities and lazinesses and evasions and pretences of the oh-dear-crying past – oh, the mountainously pretentious want – and to say only what I think and feel now at this moment which, deep down, has been the same long moment for a year and more. But why do you want to hear from me? and how do I know that you do? I don't know, but I hope. Will you write and say that you still want to hear? to see me? And come to London – I'm going back tomorrow – or let me come to you. I can come anywhere. At any time. Tomorrow.

Thank you for your card at Christmas. Such a nice, prim, nothing-at-all remark it is – 'thank you for your card at Christmas' – to end an inarticulate little letter on; because I must end, because I do not yet know if, after such a silent time, you want me to go on or want to see me. Perhaps you've forgotten. I am short, snub, unsteady, moles on my cheek, in a check suit. Of you I have only the still picture from the silliest film in the world, which is still the best film for the one reason that it allows me to send you now, with all my heart, my love.

Dylan

CAITLIN THOMAS

June 24, 1945 — 26 Paulton Square SW3

My dear my dear my dear Caitlin my love I love you; even writing, from a universe and a star and ten thousand miles away, the name, your name, CAITLIN, just makes me love you, not more, because that is impossible, darling, I have always loved you more every day since I first saw you looking silly and golden and much much too good forever for me, in that nasty place in worse-than-Belsen London, no, not more, but deeper, oh my sweetheart I love you and love me dear Cat because we are the same, we are the same, we are the one thing, the constant thing, oh dear dear Cat.

I'm writing this in bed in Constantine's and Tony's at about one o'clock Sunday morning – I mean after midnight. You are the most beautiful girl that has ever lived, and it is worth dying to have kissed you. Oh Cat, I need & want you too, I want to come to you, I must be with you, there is no life, no nothing, without you: I've told you, before, in the quiet, in the Cardy dark, by the sea, that I adored you and you thought it was a word. I do. I do, my love, my beautiful. I can see your hair now though I can't see it; & feel your breasts against my stupid body; I can hear your voice though you aren't speaking except to – who? Mary? Bloody Mary? Did you see the thing in News of the World? 'Among those not to be congratulated after the trial were Cat Thomas & her vile Dylan who loves her so much he is alone alone in a big room in London in England and yet he lets her live 300 miles away.' Oh, be near me, tonight, now, Sunday, 300 miles away. I kiss you. I love you.

I'll try to come back Wed or Thur but may have to put it off until the end of the week. I've been told of a few flats & houses & am looking for them. Now I must try to sleep because I can only say I Love You My Own Heart My Little One Caitlin my Wife and Love & Eternity.

X Dylan

Monday morning.

Still in bed. About eight o'clock in the morning. Found it terribly hard to sleep. Said your name a thousand times, my little dear. In a few minutes I'll get up and go to work: to write, still, about Allied Strategy in Burma: oh why can't they get someone else.

Tony has promised that *she* will look, for us, at the few addresses of flats I've been given. I'm thinking it is by far the best thing to get a very temporary furnished flat – however not nice – rather than an unfurnished one; so that we can leave it any time we raise enough money to go to America. I'll let you know if anything comes of it. I've been doing very little except work with Eldridge & Donald; anyway, I've only been here two days. Leaving you was like cutting my body in half; and yours. I LOVE YOU. That's as sure as the earth's turning, as the beastliness of London, as the fact that you are beautiful, as that I love Aeronwy and Llewelyn too – Caitlin my own my dear – Wire me TEM 5420 to say if you want to speak on the telephone to me. I'm going to the Zoo tomorrow, with a Lilliput photographer, to write captions for his pictures: What Animals Think. I don't know if it's Brandt; rather hope not. If they commission me straight away, I'll send on half the money. I think, by the way, that our court expenses will be sent to me at Majoda. If they are, you'll be okay. Wire or phone me about it. I'll come back as soon as I can: certainly this week. I am longing for you. That's such a little understatement. I want you. You're the whole of my life. The Rest is nothing. Believe me, Cat, forever, and write or wire & phone & let me hear your voice because I love you. I want to be in your arms.

Always & always and always & always

X

Dylan

EDITH SITWELL

Edith Sitwell had been an early supporter of Thomas's work, but he had rather neglected the friendship. This letter was in response to recent praise and an attempt to rekindle a profitable relationship.

March 31, 1946 c/o A J P Taylor Holywell Ford Oxford

Dear Miss Sitwell,

It's nine or ten years, I think, since I last met you, though we did write some letters after that; it is, anyway, a long long time, and all that time I've very much missed being able to write to you occasionally and to send you poems and to ask you about them, for I value, with all my heart, what you have said about them in the past. I find it so easy to get lost, in my actions and my words, and I know that, deeply lost so many times, I could have, through writing to you and through your writing, come somehow out and up, so much less sufferingly than I did, into the miraculous middle of the world again.

I think that, in some way, I offended you, through some thoughtless, irresponsible written or spoken word, on some occasion, those nine or ten years back. And I can't forgive myself that I can't remember what, exactly, the offence was, how crude or ignorant. Whatever it was, it seemed to stop, as though for ever, our writing to one another, let alone our meeting. May I say, now, as I know I should have said many years before, how sorry and, inarticulately, more than that, I am that some minor (oh, I hope so, minor) beastliness of mine, presumption, conceit, gaucherie, seeming-ingratitude, foul manner, callow pretension, or worse, yes, indeed, or far worse, interrupted our friendship, just beginning, and lost for so long, to me, the happiness and honour of being able to send my work, as it was written, to you, and to write to you of the never-ending-circling problems and doubts of craft and meaning and heart that must always besiege us. If my apology, true as my love of your Song of the Cold, reads to you as stiltedly as, quickly writing, it sounds to me, I'm sorry again and can only say how hard I find it to move naturally into the long silence between now and nine beautiful, dreadful years ago.

I'm daring to write to you now because I have been reading, in Our Time, your passages, or message, about my new poems, all those words glowing out of the paper like caves and eyes, full of understanding and mysteries: – though that may sound, God knows, affected, but how can I say how profoundly I was moved by the expression of your profound & loving understanding of the poems I've worked upon for so long and through so many giant and pygmy doubts, high and low darknesses, ghastly errors and exaltations? The poems you liked least were of course the worst in the book: they were worked at intermittently, out of changing values, there was no cohesion in them, poems of bits, or bits of poetry sliced off at the intellectual end of a series of conflicting, locked, and lost-before-they-were-begun, arguments. 'Paper and Sticks' was a 'light relief' where none was wanted; and I am always light as a hippo. But your quickening to the best of the poems came across to me like a new life of sympathy and mystery; to share the joy you express at the joyful poem, Fern Hill, is a new joy to me, as real as that which made the words come, at last, out of a never-to-be-buried childhood in heaven or Wales.

I hope you will write to me, forgive me for a long-gone never-meant boorish blunder or worse. Am I better now, I can ask only the never-telling tides of war and peace and duties around me? I hope you will let me meet you again.

For months and months and grey months I've been basemented in London. Now we can stay here, in a kind of summerhouse by the river, for a few green months (I trust). We are so miserably poor, blast and blast it, but the spring's singing all over the place, and, between scraping and hacking and howling at my incompetence, I've time to listen and, soon perhaps, to work again. 'Fern Hill' was the last poem I've written, in September, in Carmarthenshire, near the farm where it happened. I want very very much to write again. And I should like to write to tell you how I feel about all your poems written during the war, if one day I am forgiven and I may. There is no: 'There is no need to say what I feel about poems whose beauty is true and strange and clear to all *and* the blind'. There's always need to say what great work means to one man, how your creation of revelation and his revealed acceptance meet in a point – did Yeats say it? – of light.

But I've written enough and too much – pass over, if you

can, all the tongue-knotted awkwardnesses, these stammers for nine years back – and I must wait now hoping, all the time, to hear from you.

Yours sincerely,
Dylan Thomas

CAITLIN THOMAS

January or February, 1948 Blaen Cwm Llangain

Caitlin, my own, my dear, my darling whom I love forever: Here it's snowbound, dead, dull, damned; there's hockey-voiced Nancy being jolly over pans and primuses in the kitchen, and my father trembling and moaning all over the place, crying out sharply when the dog barks – Nancy's dog – weeping, despairing. My mother, in the Infirmary, with her leg steel-splinted up towards the ceiling and a 300 lb weight hanging from it, is good and cheerful and talks without stop about the removed ovaries, dropped wombs, amputated breasts, tubercular spines, & puerperal fevers of her new friends in the women's surgical ward. She will have to lie, trussed, on her back with her leg weighted, for at least two months, and then will be a long time learning, like a child, to walk again. The doctors have stuck a great steel pin right through her knee, so that, by some method, the broken leg will grow to the same length as the other one. My father, more nervous & harrowed than I have ever seen him, cannot stay on here alone, & Nancy cannot stay with him, so she will take him back with her to Brixham to stay, until my Mother can leave the Infirmary. My Mother will therefore be alone in the Infirmary for months. No-one here will look after the dog Mably, & Nancy cannot take him back to her tiny cottage as she has, already, a Labrador retriever: they didn't know what to do but to have

Mabli destroyed, which is wrong, because he is young & well and very nice. So I have said that I will take him.

My darling, I love you. I loved you, if that is possible, more than ever in my life, and I have always loved you. When you left, going upstairs in the restaurant with that old horror, I sat for a long time lost lost lost, oh Caitlin sweetheart I love you. I don't understand how I can behave to you senselessly, foully, brutally, as though you were not the most beautiful person on the earth and the one I love forever. The train hourly took me further & further away from you and from the only thing I want in the world. The train was icy, and hours late. I waited hours, in Carmarthen Station in the early snowing morning, for a car to take me to Misery Cottage. All the time, without stopping, I thought of you, and of my foulness to you, and of how I have lost you. Oh Cat Cat please, my dear, don't let me lose you. Let me come back to you. Come back to me. I can't live without you. There's nothing left then. I can't ask you to forgive me, but I can say that I will never again be a senseless, horrible, dulled beast like that. I love you.

I am leaving here, snowbound or not, on Tuesday, & will reach London early Tuesday evening, with bag & Mably. I could come straightaway to you if – if you will have me. Christ, aren't we each other's? This time, this last time, darling, I promise you I shall not again be like that. You're beautiful. I love you. Oh, this Blaencwm room. Fire, pipe, whining, nerves, Sunday joint, wireless, no beer until one in the morning, death. And you aren't here. I think of you all the time, in snow, in bed.

Dylan

MARGARET TAYLOR

Margaret Taylor incurred the exasperation of her husband, the historian A. J. P. Taylor, over her espousal of the feckless young poet she first met in Wales when he was just twenty years old. Despite opposition, she continued to patronise and support Dylan, and later the Thomas family. She it was who found and provided the house at Laugharne in which Dylan spent the last years of his life. His feelings towards her were equivocal. There was no romance between them but in his letters he often needed to call upon his most lyrical flights of gratitude and, occasionally, remorse.

May 11, 1949 Boat House, Laugharne

My dear Margaret,

I should have written. I have been meaning to write each day. I've been wanting to write, but have put it off and off. Oh, all those bells were cracked long ago! They ring like dustbins! But it's true that each day since coming to this place I love and where I want to work (my own) already, I've been saying to my contemptible self, You must write to Margaret at once to say that this is *it*: the place, the house, the workroom, the time. I can never thank you enough for making this fresh beginning possible by all the trust you have put in me, by all the gifts you have made me, by all your labour & anxiety in face of callous & ungrateful behaviour. I know that the only way to express my deep deep gratitude is to be happy & to write. Here I am happy and writing. All I shall write in this water and tree room on the cliff, every word, will be my thanks to you. I hope to God it will be good enough. I'll send you all I write. And ordinary letters too, full of trees & water & gossip &

no news. This isn't that kind of letter. This is only the expression of the greatest gratitude in the world: you have given me a life. And now I am going to live it.

Dylan

CAITLIN THOMAS

February 25, 1950 22 East 38th Street New York

My darling far-away love, my precious Caitlin, my wife dear, I love you as I have never loved you, oh please remember me all day & every day as I remember you here in this terrible, beautiful, dream and nightmare city which would only be any good at all if we were together in it, if every night we clung together in it. I love you, Cat, my Cat, your body, heart, soul, everything, and I am always and entirely yours.

How are you, my dear? When did you go with Ivy back to Laugharne? I hope you didn't racket about too much because that makes you as ill as racketing makes me. And how is my beloved Colum and sweet fiend Aeron? Give them my love, please. I will myself write to Llewelyn over this weekend when I temporarily leave New York and go to stay with John Brinnin – a terribly nice man – in his house in the country an hour or so away. And how are the old ones? I'll write to them, too. I love you, I can see you, now this minute, your face & body, your beautiful hair, I can hear your lovely, un-understandable voice. I love you, & I love our children, & I love our house. Here, each night I have to take things to sleep: I am staying right in the middle of Manhattan, surrounded by skyscrapers infinitely taller & stranger than one has ever known from the pictures: I am staying in a room, an hotel room for the promised flat did not come off, on the 30th floor: and the *noise* all day &

night: without some drug, I couldn't sleep at all. The hugest, heaviest lorries, police-cars, firebrigades, ambulances, all with their banshee sirens wailing & screaming, seem never to stop; Manhattan is built on rock, a lot of demolition work is going on to take up yet another super Skyscraper, & so there is almost continuous dynamite blasting. Aeroplanes just skim the tips of the great glimmering skyscrapers, some beautiful, some hellish. And I have no idea what on earth I am doing here in the very loud, mad middle of the last mad Empire on earth: – except to think of you, & love you, & to work for us. I have done two readings this week, to the Poetry Center of New York: each time there was an audience of about a thousand. I felt a very lonely, foreign midget orating up there, in a huge hall, before all those faces; but the readings went well. After this country weekend, where I arrange with Brinnin some of the rest of my appallingly extensive programme, I go to Harvard University, Cambridge, Boston, for about 2 days, then to Washington, then back to New York, then, God knows, I daren't think, but I know it includes Yale, Princeton, Vassar – 3 big universities, as you know, old know-all, – & Salt Lake City, where the Mormons live, & Notre Dame, the Jesuit College, & the middle West, Iowa, Ohio, Chicago – & Florida, the kind of exotic resort, & after that the mere thought makes my head roar like New York. To the places near to New York, Brinnin is driving me by car; to others I go by myself by train; to the more distant places, I fly. But *whatever* happens, by God I don't fly back. Including landing at Dublin, Canada, & Boston, for very short times, I was in the air, cooped up in the stratosphere, for 17 hours with 20 of the nastiest people in the sky. I had an awful hangover from our London do as well; the terrible height makes one's ears hurt like hell, one's lips chap, one's belly turn; and it went on forever. I'm coming back by boat.

I've been to a few parties, met lots of American poets, writers, critics, hangers-on, some very pleasant, all furiously polite & hospitable. But, apart from on one occasion, I've stuck nearly all the time to American beer, which, though thin, I like a lot & is ice-cold. I arrived, by the way, on the coldest day New York had had for years & years: It was 4 above zero. You'd have loved it. I never thought anything could be so cold, my ears nearly fell off: the wind just whipped through that monstrous duffle. But, as soon as I got into a room, the steamed heat was worse: I think I can stand zero better than that, &, to the astonishment of natives, I keep all windows open to the top. I've been, too, to lots of famous places: up the top of the Empire State Building, the tallest there is, which terrified me so much, I had to come down at once; to Greenwich Village a feebler Soho but with stronger drinks; & this morning John Brinnin is driving us to Harlem. I say 'us', you see: in the same hotel as me is staying our old New Zealander, Allen Curnow, & I see quite a bit of him. I've met Auden, & Oscar Williams, a very odd, but kind, little man.

And now it must look to you, my Cat, as though I am enjoying myself here. I'm not. It's nightmare, night & day; there never was such a place; I would never get used to the speed, the noise, the utter indifference of the crowds, the frightening politeness of the intellectuals, and, most of all, these huge phallic towers, up & up & up, hundreds of floors, into the impossible sky. I feel so terrified of this place, I hardly dare to leave my hotelroom – luxurious – until Brinnin or someone calls for me. Everybody uses the telephone all the time: it is like breathing: it is now nine o'clock in the morning, & I've had six calls: all from people whose names I did not catch to invite me to a little poity at an address I had no idea of. And most of all most of all most of all, though, God, there's no need to say this to you who understand everything, I want to be with you. If we could be here together, everything would be allright. *Never* again would I come here, or to any far place, without you; but especially never to here. The rest of America may be all right, & perhaps I can understand it, but that is the last monument there is to the insane desire for power that shoots its buildings up to the stars & roars its engines louder & faster than they have ever been roared before and makes everything cost the earth & where the imminence of death is reflected in every last powerstroke and grab of the great money bosses, the big shots, the multis, one never sees. This morning we go down to see the other side beyond the skyscrapers: black Harlem, starving Jewish East Side. A family of four in New York is very very poor on £14 a week. I'll buy some nylons all the same next week, & some tinned stuff. Anything else?

Last-minute practicalities: How does the money go? Have any new bills arrived. If so, send them, when you write (& write soon my dear love, my sweetheart, that is all I wait for except to come home to you) to the address on the kitchen wall. I enclose a cheque to Phil Raymond, & an open cheque to Gleed; pay that bill when you can.

Remember me. I love you. Write to me.

Your loving, loving Dylan

March 11, 1950 1669 Thirty-first Street Washington

Kiss Colum again. Put your hand on your heart for me

I shall write lots & lots & lots to you from now, on the endless trains.

Caitlin my own own own dearest love whom God and *my* love and *your* love for me protect, my sweet wife, my dear one, my Irish heart, my wonderful wonderful girl who is with me invisibly every second of these dreadful days, awake or sleepless, who is forever and forever with me and is my own true beloved amen – I love you, I need you, I want, want you, we have never been apart as long as this, never, never, and we will never be again. I am writing to you now, lying in bed, in the Roman Princess's sister's rich social house, in a posh room that is hell on earth. Oh why, why, *didn't* we arrange it *somehow* that we came out together to this devastating, insane, demoniacally loud, roaring continent. We *could* somehow have arranged it. Why oh why did I think I could live, I could bear to live, I could think of living, for all these torturing, unending, echoing months without you, Cat, my life, my wife, my wife on earth and in God's eyes, my reason for my blood, breath, and bone. Here, in this vast, mad horror, that doesn't know its size, or its strength, or its weakness, or its barbaric speed, stupidity, din, selfrighteousness, this cancerous Babylon, here we could cling together, sane, safe, & warm & face, together, everything. I LOVE YOU. I have been driven for what seem like, and probably are, thousands of miles, along neoned, jerrybuilt, motel-ed, turbined, ice-cream-salooned, gigantically hoarded roads of the lower region of the damned, from town to town, college to college, university to university, hotel to hotel, & all I want, before Christ, before you, is to hold you in my arms in our house in Laugharne, Carmarthenshire. And the worst, by a thousand miles – no, thousands & thousands & thousands of miles – is to come. I have touched only the nearest-together of my eternally foreign dates. Tomorrow, I go back from Washington, hundreds of miles, to New York. There I talk to Columbia University. The very next day I start on my pilgrimage, my *real* pilgrimage, of the damned. I go to Iowa, Idaho, Indiana, Salt Lake City, & then a titanic distance to Chicago. All alone. Friend Brinnin leaves me at New York. And from Chicago I fly to San Francisco, & from there I lurch, blinded with smoke and noise, to Los Angeles. The distance from New York – where I shall be tomorrow – to Los Angeles is further than the distance from London to New York. Oh, Cat, my beautiful, my love, what am I doing here? I am no globe-trotter, no cosmopolitan, I have no desire to hurl across the American nightmare like one of their damned motorcars. I want to live quietly, with you & Colum, & noisily with Aeronwy, & I want to see Llewelyn, & I want to sit in my hut and write, & I want to eat your stews, and I want to touch your breasts and cunt, and I want every night to lie, in love & peace, close, close, close, close, close to you, closer than the marrow of your soul. I LOVE YOU.

Everything is not terrible here. I have met many kind, intelligent, humorous people, & a few, a very few, who hate the American scene, the driving lust for success, the adulation of power, as much as I do. There is more food than I dreamt of. And I want to tell you again, my Cat, that I still drink nothing but ice-cold beer. I don't touch spirits at all, though that is all that anyone else seems to drink – & in enormous quantity. But if I touched anything else but beer I just *couldn't* manage to get along. I couldn't face this world if I were ill. I have to remain, outwardly, as strong as possible. It is only in my heart and head that the woes and the terrors burn. I miss you a million million times more than if my arms, legs, head, & trunk were all cut off. You *are* my body, & I am yours. Holily & sacredly, & lovingly & lustfully, spiritually, & to the very deeps of the unconscious sea, I love you, Caitlin my wild wise wonderful woman, my girl, the mother of our Colum cauliflower. Your letter I read ten times a day, in cars, trains, pubs, in the street, in bed. I think I know it by heart. Of *course* I know it by heart. Your heart, alive, leaping, & loving, is in every word. Thank you, my dear, for your lovely letter. Please write as often as you can. And I will write too. I have not written since my first letter because never for a second, except for falling, trembling & exhausted thinking, thinking, thinking, of you, have I stopped travelling or reading aloud on stages and platforms. This is the first day on which I have had no work to do. I waited until I was in bed until I wrote to you. I can cry on the pillow then, and say your name across the miles that sever you from me. I LOVE YOU. Please, love & remember me & WAIT FOR ME. Keep the stew waiting on the fire for me. Kiss Calico Colum for me, & arrant Aeron.

I hope you got the stockings I sent you. I sent a pair to Ivy too. Today I had sent from a big shop in Washington lots of chocolates, sweets, & candies, for you, for Aeron, for my mother. Darling darling, I am sorry I could do nothing for dear Aeron's birthday. Dates & time were a maze of speed & noise as I drove like a sweating, streamlined, fat, redfaced comet along the *incredible* roads. But tell her many sweets & things shd reach her in a few days. From N York tomorrow, I shall also send some foodstuffs.

About the Ungoed cheque: if my chequebook is in the bottom of my suitcase, I shall write him a cheque & put it into this letter when I post it tomorrow. If it is not in my suitcase, but in my other suitcase in Brinnin's house, I shall send it separately tomorrow. I cannot look in the case now. It is downstairs. The house is dark. I shall lie here & love you. I DO Love You, Angel. Be good to me & ours.

What can I say to you that I have not said a thousand times before, dear dear Cat? It is: I love you.

March 15, 1950 c/o Brinnin Valley Road
Westport Conn

from your lost, loving Dylan.

Darling my dear my Cat,

I love you.

You're mine for always as for always I am yours. I love you. I have been away for just over 3 weeks, & there's never been a longer & sadder time since the Flood. Oh write soon, my love, my Irish, my Colum's mother, my beautiful golden dear. There isn't a moment of any insane day when I do not feel you loving and glowing, when I do not grieve for you, for me, for us both, my sweetheart, when I do not long to be with you as deep as the sea. Only three weeks! Oh God, oh God, how much longer. I wrote you last from be-Bibbled Washington. Then back I sweated to New York. Then I read in Columbia University, New York. Then I flew to Cornell University, read, caught a night-sleeper-train to Ohio, arriving this morning. This evening, in an hour's time, I do my little act at Kenyon University, then another night-train, this time to Chicago. I never seem to sleep in a bed any more, only on planes & trains. I'm hardly living; I'm just a voice on wheels. And the damndest thing is that quite likely I may arrive home with hardly any money at all, both the United States *and* Great Britain taxing my earnings – my earnings for us, Colum, Aeron, Llewelyn, for our house that makes me cry to think of, for the water, the heron, old sad empty Brown's. I am writing this in a room in Kenyon University, & can find no paper or sharp pencil & am too scared to go out and find somebody to ask. As soon as I raise the courage, I shall write Ungoed's cheque – it wasn't, of course, in my suitcase in Washington at all but in Brinnin's possession in N York – & address the envelope & have the letter air-mailed. I love you. Every *second* I think of and love you. Remember me. Write quickly. You are all I have on earth.

Did you get nylons & candy?

And please, when you write, tell me how the money's going at home, how you are making out.

Kiss Colum & Aeron for me.

Have you thought of having Mary Keene or Oxford Elizabeth down?

Tell me everything.

Love me, my dear love Cat.

Be good.

Write quickly. What can I send you?

I LOVE YOU XXX

Found a razorblade to sharpen my pencil, but no more paper. Out on the grounds – they call it the campus – of this

College the undergraduates, looking more like bad actors out of an American co-ed film, are strolling, running, baseballing, in every variety of fancy-dress. Someone in the building is playing jazz on an out-of-date piano: the saddest sound. In a few minutes now I go out for cocktails with the President. I do not want to have cocktails with any President. I want to be home. I want you. I want you with my heart and my body because I love you. Perhaps, perhaps, perhaps, the door may suddenly open & in you will come: like the sun. But I do not think it likely. I love you, my pet.

March 16, 1950 The Quadrangle Club Chicago

Cat: my cat: If only you would write to me: My love, oh Cat. This is not, as it seems from the address above, a dive, joint, saloon, etc, but the honourable & dignified headquarters of the dons of the University of Chicago. I love you. That is all I know. But all I know, too, is that I am writing into space: the kind of dreadful, unknown space I am just going to enter. I am going to Iowa, Illinois, Idaho, Indindiana, but these, though misspelt, *are* on the map. You are not. Have you forgotten me? I am the man you used to say you loved. I used to sleep in your arms – do you remember? But you never write. You are perhaps mindless of me. I am not of you. I love you. There isn't a moment of any hideous day when I do not say to myself, 'It will be alright. I shall go home. Caitlin loves me. I love Caitlin.' But perhaps you have forgotten. If you have forgotten, or lost your affection for me, please, my Cat, let me know. I Love You.

Dylan

April 5, 1950 c/o Witt-Diamant 1520 Willard St
San Francisco

My love my Caitlin my love my love

thank you (I love you) for your beautiful beautiful beautiful letter and (my love) for the love you sent. Please forgive, Cat dear, the nasty little note I sent about your not-writing: it was only because I was so worried and so deeply in love with you. This is going to be the shortest letter because I am writing it on a rocking train that is taking me from San Francisco – the best city on earth – to Vancouver in Canada. And with this tiny, but profoundly loving, letter, I also send you a cheque to Magdalen College for £50 & a cheque for £15 to you: that £15 seems an odd amount, but God knows how much is in the Chelsea bank. I unfortunately can't find the Dathan Davies bill you sent, so can you pay it out of this. Please, my own sweetheart, send all the bills & troubles to me after this. And I hope the cheques are met. The train is going so fast through wonderful country along the pacific coast that I can write no more. As soon as I get on stationary land I will write longly. I said San Francisco was the best city on earth. It is incredibly beautiful, all hills and bridges and blinding blue sky and boats and the Pacific ocean. I am trying – & there's every reason to believe it will succeed – to arrange that you & me & Colum (my Colum, your Colum,) come to San Francisco next spring when I will become, for six months, a professor in the English department of the University. You will love it here. I am madly unhappy but I love it here. I am desperate for you but I *know* that we can, together, come here. I love you. I love you. I love you. I am glad you are stiff & staid. I am rather overwrought but am so much in love with you that it does not matter. I spent last evening with Varda, the Greek painter, who remembers you when you were fifteen. I wish I did. A long letter tomorrow. O my heart, my golden heart, how I miss you. There's an intolerable emptiness in me, that can be made whole only by your soul & body. I will come back alive & as deep in love with you as a cormorant dives, as an anemone grows, as Neptune breathes, as the sea is deep. God bless & protect you & Llewelyn & Aeron & Colum, my, our, Colum. I love you.

Dylan

P.S. Write, air mail, to the above address. I return to S. Francisco in a week.
P.S.S. Darling, I realise fifteen pounds is inadequate, but let that big £50 get thro' the bank alright & then I can send more. I can send you a cheque in dollars next week, which you can cash through the account of my poor old man or through Ivy.

I love you.

April 7, 1950

Caitlin. Just to write down your name like that. Caitlin. I don't have to say My dear, My darling, my sweetheart, though I do say those words, to you in myself, all day and night. Caitlin. And all the words are in that one word. Caitlin, Caitlin, and I can see your blue eyes and your golden hair and your slow smile and your faraway voice. Your faraway voice is saying, now, at my ear, the words you said in your last letter, and thank you, dear, for the love you said and sent. I love you. Never forget that, for one single moment of the long, slow, sad Laugharne day, never forget it in your mazed trances, in your womb & your bones, in our bed at night. I love you. Over this continent I take your love inside me, your love goes with me up in the aeroplaned air, into all the hotel bedrooms where momentarily I open my bag – half full, as ever, of dirty shirts – and lay down my head & do not sleep until dawn because I can hear your heart beat beside me, your voice saying my name and our love above the noise of the night-traffic, above the neon flashing, deep in my loneliness, my love.

Today is Good Friday. I am writing this in an hotel bedroom in Vancouver, British Columbia, Canada, where yesterday I gave two readings, one in the university, one in the ballroom of the Vancouver Hotel, and made one broadcast. Vancouver is on the sea, and gigantic mountains doom above it. Behind the mountains lie other mountains, lies an unknown place, 30,000 miles of mountainous wilderness, the lost land of Columbia where cougars live and black bears. But the city of Vancouver is a quite handsome hellhole. It is, of course, being Canadian, more British than Cheltenham. I spoke last night – or read, I never lecture, how could I? – in front of two huge union jacks. The pubs – they are called beer-parlours – serve only beer, are not allowed to have whiskey or wine or any spirits at all – and are open only for a few hours a day. There are, in this monstrous hotel, two bars, one for Men, one for Women. They do not mix. Today, Good Friday, nothing is open nor will be open all day long. Everybody is pious and patriotic, apart from a few people in the university & my old friend Malcolm Lowry – do you remember Under the Volcano – who lives in a hut in the mountains & who came down to see me last night. Do you remember his wife Margery? We met her with Bill & Helen in Richmond, and, later, I think, in Oxford. She, anyway, remembers you well and sends you her love.

This afternoon I pick up my bag of soiled clothes and take a plane to Seattle. And thank God to be out of British Canada & back in the terrible United States of America. I read poems to the University there tonight. And then I have one day's rest in Seattle, & then on Sunday I fly to Montana, where the cowboys are, thousands of them, tell Ebie, and then on Monday I fly – it takes about 8 hours – to Los Angeles & Hollywood: the nightmare zenith of my mad, lonely tour.

But oh, San Francisco! It is and has everything. Here in Canada, five hours away by plane, you wouldn't think that such a place as San Francisco could exist. The wonderful sunlight there, the hills, the great bridges, the Pacific at your shoes. Beautiful Chinatown. Every race in the world. The sardine fleets sailing out. The little cable-cars whizzing down the city hills. The lobsters, clams, & crabs. Oh, Cat, what food for you. Every kind of seafood there is. And all the people are open and friendly. And next year we both come to live there, you & me & Colum & maybe Aeron. This is sure. I am offered a job in two universities. When I return to San Francisco next week, after Los Angeles, for another two readings, I shall know definitely which of the jobs to take. The pay will be enough to keep us comfortably, though no more. Everyone connected with the Universities is hard-up. But that doesn't matter. Seafood is cheap. Chinese food is cheaper, & lovely. Californian wine is good. The iced bock beer is good. What more? And the city is built on hills; it dances in the sun for nine months of the year; & the Pacific Ocean never runs dry.

Last week I went to Big Sur, a mountainous region by the sea, and stayed the night with Henry Miller. Tell Ivy that; she who hid his books in the oven. He lives about 6,000 feet up in the hills, over the blinding blue Pacific, in a hut of his own making. He has married a pretty young Polish girl, & they have two small children. He is gentle and mellow and gay.

I love you, Caitlin.

You asked me about the shops. I only know that the shops in the big cities, in New York, Chicago, San Francisco, are full of everything you have ever heard of and also full of everything one has never heard of or seen. The foodshops knock you down. All the women are smart, as in magazines – I mean, the women in the main streets; behind, lie the eternal poor, beaten, robbed, humiliated, spat upon, done to death – and slick & groomed. But they are not as beautiful as you. And when you & me are in San Francisco, you will be smarter & slicker than them, and the sea & sun will make you jump over the roofs & the trees, & you will never be tired again. Oh, my lovely dear, how I love you. I love you for ever & ever. I see you every moment of the day & night. I see you in our little house, tending the pomegranate of your eye. I love you. Kiss Colum, kiss Aeron & Llewelyn. Is Elisabeth with you? Remember me to her. I love you. Write, write, write, write, my sweetheart Caitlin. Write to me still c/o Brinnin; though the letters come late that way, I am sure of them. Do not despair. Do not be too tired. Be always good to me. I shall one day be in your arms, my own, however shy we shall be. Be good to me, as I am always to you. I love you. Think of us together in the San Franciscan sun, which we shall be. I love you. I want you. Oh, darling, when I was with you all the time, how did I ever shout at you? I love you. Think of me.

Your
Dylan

I enclose a cheque for £15.
I will write from Hollywood in three days.
I will send some more money.
I love you.

January or February 1951 — Isfahan Iran

Caitlin dear,

Your letter, as it was meant to, made me want to die. I did not think that, after reading it so many times till I knew every pain by heart, I could go on with these days and nights, alone with my loneliness – now, as I know too well, for ever – and knowing that, a long way and a lifetime away, you no longer loved or wanted me. (After your cold, disliking letter, you wrote: 'All my love, Caitlin.' You could have spared that irony.) But the bloody animal always *does* go on. Now I move through these days in a kind of dumb, blind despair, and slowly every day ends. It's the nights I fear most, when the despair breaks down, is dumb and blind no longer, and I am only myself in the dark. I am only alone in an unknown room in a strange town in a benighted country, without any pretences and crying like a fool. Last night I saw you smiling, glad, at me, as you did a thousand years ago; and I howled like the jackals outside. Then, in the morning, it was the same again: walking, in despair, frozen, over a desert. It was even a real desert, the camels aloof, the hyenas laughing. I'm writing this, perhaps last, letter, just before I go to bed in an hotel full of brutes. If only I didn't have to go to bed. Nobody here, in this writing room, the wireless shouting Persian, can see anything wrong with me. I'm only a little fat foreigner writing a letter: a loving, happy letter to his wife 'waiting at home'. Christ, if they knew. If they knew that the woman I am writing to no longer needs me, has shut her heart & her body against me, although she is my life. I cannot live without you – you, always – and I have no intention of doing so. I fly back, from Tehran to London, on, I am almost certain, the 14th of February. I shall cable you from Tehran the time of my arrival. You said, before we parted, that you would come up to London to meet me on my return. You will not, I suppose, be doing that now? If you are not, will you please – it is not a great deal to ask – leave a message at the McAlpines. I will not come back to Laugharne until I know that I am wanted: not as an inefficient mispayer of bills, but as myself and for you. If you do not meet me in London, I shall ring the McAlpines. If there is no message there from you, I shall know that everything is over. It is very terrible writing this such a great distance from you. In a few minutes I shall go to my bedroom, climb into bed in my shirt, and think of you. The bedroom knows your name well, as do many bedrooms in this country. 'Caitlin, Caitlin', I will say, and you will come drifting to me, clear & beautiful, until my eyes blur and you are gone. I love you. Oh, darling Cat, I love you.

Dylan

MARGED HOWARD-STEPNEY

Marged Howard-Stepney was a rich woman of Welsh origin. She had had a chequered life and in her thirties suffered from drink and nerves. But she was generous to Dylan. This letter was probably never sent, but it was seen by Caitlin. Dylan's attempt to smooth Caitlin's disgusted feathers follows.

1952

My dear Marged, You told me, once, upon a time, to call on you when I was beaten down, and you would try to pick me up. Maybe I should not have remembered

You told me, once, to call on you
When I was beaten down...

Dear Marged,

Once upon a time you told me,
I remember in my bones,
That when the bad world had rolled me
Over on the scolding stones,
Shameless, lost, as the day I came
I should with my beggar's cup
Howl down the wind and call your name
And you, you would raise me up.

The same very same time I told you,
And swore by my heart & head,

That I would forever hold you
To the lovely words you said;
I never thought so soon I'd lie
Lonely in the whining dust;
My one wish is to love and die,
But life is all mustn't & must.

I mustn't love, & I must die
But only when I am told,
And Fear sits in the mansioned sky
And the winged Conventions scold,
And Money is the dunghill King
And his royal nark is the dun;
And dunned to death I write this jingling thing
Dunned to death in the dear sun.
This jingling thing

CAITLIN THOMAS

Caitlin,

Please read this.

That letter you saw was horrible, it was dirty and cadging and lying. You know it was horrible, dirty, and cadging and lying. There was no truth in it. There was no truth meant to be in it. It was vile, a conscientious piece of contrived bamboozling dirt, which *nobody* was supposed to see – not you, or that Marged gin woman. I wrote it as I will tell you. The fact that you read it has made me so full of loathing & hatred for myself, and despair, that I haven't been able to speak to you. I haven't been able to speak to you about it. There was nothing I could say except, It isn't true, it's foul, sponging lies. And how could I say that when you'd *seen* it? How could I tell you it was all lies, that it was all made up for nothing, when you'd seen the dirty words? You'd say, If you didn't mean the dirty words, why did you write them?

And all I could answer would be, Because I wanted to see what foul dripping stuff I could hurt myself to write in order to fawn for money. I'd as soon post that muck as I'd swim, I was going to tear it up in a million bloody bits. Marged told me, when she was drunk with that Pritchard, to write to her about what I owed the Insurance things & others, or that's what I gathered – as much as anyone could gather. Or perhaps that's what I wanted to gather. Anyway, I put the Insurance thing summons in an envelope & explained, in a note, that I'd spent the other half of the money she'd given us for that, & that there were other real debts too. Then I went on writing something else – those endless rotten verses of mine, which I almost agree with you about – and then, when I came to a dead bit, to a real awful jam in the words, I saw – on the other broken table – when I'd written to Marged & started writing a proper sycophantic arse-licking hell letter, putting in pretentious bits, introducing heart-throb lies, making, or trying to make, a foul beggar's lie-book of it. I only just avoided tuberculosis & orphans. There's no excuse for my writing this. I'd no idea it would go further than the floor of this shed. I was all wrong to drivel out this laboured chicanery. So wrong, & ashamed, I haven't been able to say a word to you about it. The misery I'm in can't make up for, or explain the misery I've made for you by my callous attempt at a mock-literature of the slimiest kind.

I love you
Dylan

This poem was written for Caitlin Thomas's 39th birthday.

For Caitlin Thomas on Her Birthday
8th December 1952, from her Husband.

Caitlin I love you
And I always will.
I love you in Brown's Hotel,
The Cross House, Sir John's Hill,
London, New York, bed.
In any place, at any time,
Now, then, live, dead –

This is all that I
Have to say
On your birthday,
My Caitlin:
As sure as death is sure,
So is my love for you everlasting

ELIZABETH REITELL

Elizabeth Reitell met Dylan Thomas when he was touring the USA in 1953. She was the assistant to John Brinnin, the director of the Poetry Center in New York who had organised Dylan's visit. She was 33 when they met, and had already been married twice. They worked together on Under Milk Wood *and began an affair. When he returned to the USA in the autumn of that year, he spent his last days with her. 'I love you, but I'm alone', he told her. A few days later Dylan Thomas was dead following an alcoholic binge.*

June 16, 1953

Boat House Laugharne
but as from, privately, The Savage Club
One Carlton Terrace London SW3

Liz love,

I miss you terribly much.

The plane rode high and rocky, and over Newfoundland it swung into lightning and billiard-ball hail, and the old deaf woman next to me, on her way to Algiers via Manchester, got sick in a bag of biscuits, and the bar – a real, tiny bar – stayed open all the bourbon way. London was still glassy from Coronation Day, and for all the customs-men cared I could have packed my bags with cocaine and bits of chopped women. All my friends, including the Irish ones I stay with, were, early that morning, in the middle of Coronation parties that had already lasted a week, and did not seem to think that I had been away: my broken bone, of course they took for granted, and they showed me an assortment of cuts, black eyes, & little fractures to prove that they too had suffered for Royalty. I came back here, to the always sad West drizzle, the following week, the candies running in my bag, and have just been sitting around, getting accustomed. These are the first words I've written, and all they mean to say is: I miss you a great, great deal. We were together so much, sick, well, silly, happy, plagued, but with you I was happy all the time.

No, don't send that stupid Prologue to Richman, but please to me. And also, if you can, any other reviews and also some of the poems among the papers.

I saw my Welsh solicitor, and he did not appear to know why I had gone to see stuffy Maclean O.B.E. I told him he had written to me to ask me to go, but he said no. Who is right, if anybody, can you remember? Now he says that he intends to go on with the anti-Time case only in Europe whose libel-laws he understands, and to leave the American side altogether. I told him about that New Directions digest of reviews, on yellow paper, that you were going to send Maclean. If you haven't already sent it to Maclean, would you send it to me to give to the Welsh solicitor. If Maclean has it, he, Welsh solicitor, will write Maclean for it. And this is disjointed & probably confusing. Hope you can disentangle it. And I'm sorry, Liz dear, that, all these miles away, I am still worrying you over such small things. I wish I was worrying you, very near.

Later today – this is the wet, gray morning, all seabirds & mist and children's far-off voices and regret everywhere in the wind & rain, – I'll write to Stravinsky, and then soon may know a bit more of where I shall be & what I shall do this fall. I've been asked to go to an International Literary Conference – oh God, oh Pittsburgh – in October, with Eliot, Thomas Mann, Forster, Elizabeth Bowen, Camus, Hemingway, Wilder, Faulkner, and my agent in London says I certainly should and I probably shall. With those boys' names, there *must* be money. Oh, and Arthur Miller will be there too, so he and I can be avant-garde together and write a play in which *everybody* takes his clothes off in a sewer. It's a shame our sweet little David couldn't have had that bunch all together in his party. Remember me to little sticky-fingers if ever you see him. And to Ruthven, please? With thanks for housing my cases of rubbish. And to Mr Campbell in the bucketing rain in F. Street, and to the so liberal party, and to Herb at the Crucible, and to Charlie Read chasing you – which is more than Herbert will do this year at Harvard. And always to John, to whom I shall write this long, trembling week.

My arm is still in plaster: new Welsh plaster. I haven't yet found a Doctor like Milton, nor will I ever. All my best wishes to him: he picked me out of the sick pit with his winking needle and his witty wild way.

Oh, I miss you, Liz.

I've put 2 addresses at the top of this letter. The first is for Poetry Center. The second – deep as a grave full of comedians – for you and me should you write, one day, from you to me.

I'm sending this to Charles Street. Next month I'll write to you at Dundee.

What are you doing?

Love, love, to you,
Dylan

Discover more by Dylan Thomas

www.weidenfeldandnicolson.co.uk